instant manager
skills for success

leading
PEOPLE

PHIL BAGULEY

HODDER
EDUCATION
PART OF HACHETTE LIVRE UK

The publisher has used its best endeavours to ensure that the URLs for external websites referred to in this book are correct and active at the time of going to press. However, the publisher and the author have no responsibility for the websites and can make no guarantee that a site will remain live or that the content will remain relevant, decent or appropriate.

Orders: Please contact Bookpoint Ltd, 130 Milton Park, Abingdon, Oxon OX14 4SB. Telephone: (44) 01235 827720, Fax: (44) 01235 400454. Lines are open from 9.00 to 5.00, Monday to Saturday, with a 24-hour message answering service. You can also order through our website www.hoddereducation.co.uk.

British Library Cataloguing in Publication Data
A catalogue record for this title is available from the British Library.

ISBN-13: 978 0340 94733 3

First published	2010
Impression number	10 9 8 7 6 5 4 3 2 1
Year	2013 2012 2011 2010

Copyright © 2010 Phil Baguley

Typeset by Transet Limited, Coventry, England.
Printed in Great Britain for Hodder Education, an Hachette Livre UK Company, 338 Euston Road, London NW1 3BH, by Cox & Wyman, Reading, Berkshire RG1 8EX.

Hachette Livre UK's policy is to use papers that are natural, renewable and recyclable products and made from wood grown in sustainable forests. The logging and manufacturing processes are expected to conform to the environmental regulations of the country of origin.

The Chartered Management Institute

CMI

The Chartered Management Institute is the only chartered professional body that is dedicated to management and leadership. We are committed to raising the performance of business by championing management.

We represent 86,000 individual managers and have 450 corporate members. Within the Institute there are also a number of distinct specialisms, including the Institute of Business Consulting and Women in Management Network.

We exist to help managers tackle the management challenges they face on a daily basis by raising the standard of management in the UK. We are here to help individuals become better managers and companies develop better managers.

We do this through a wide range of products and services, from practical management checklists to tailored training and qualifications. We produce research on the latest 'hot' management issues, provide a vast array of useful information through our online management information centre, as well as offering consultancy services and career information.

You can access these resources 'off the shelf' or we can provide solutions just for you. Our range of products and services is designed to ensure organisations and managers develop their potential and excel. Whether you are at the start of your career or a proven performer in the boardroom, we have something for you.

We engage policy makers and opinion formers and, as the leading authority on management, we are regularly consulted on a range of management issues. Through our in-depth research and regular policy surveys of members, we have a deep understanding of the latest management trends.

For more information visit our website **www.managers.org.uk** or call us on **01536 207307**.

CMI

Chartered Manager

Transform the way you work

The Chartered Management Institute's Chartered Manager award is the ultimate accolade for practising professional managers. Designed to transform the way you think about your work and how you add value to your organisation, it is based on demonstrating measurable impact.

This unique award proves your ability to make a real difference in the workplace.

Chartered Manager focuses on the six vital business skills of:

- Leading people
- Managing change
- Meeting customer needs
- Managing information and knowledge
- Managing activities and resources
- Managing yourself

Transform your organisation

There is a clear and well-established link between good management and improved organisational performance. Recognising this, the Chartered Manager scheme requires individuals to demonstrate how they are applying their leadership and change management skills to make significant impact within their organisation.

Transform your career

Whatever career stage a manager is at Chartered Manager will set them apart. Chartered Manager has proven to be a stimulus to career progression, either via recognition by their current employer or through the motivation to move on to more challenging roles with new employers.

But don't take just our word for it ...
Chartered Manager has transformed the careers and organisations of managers in all sectors.

- *'Being a Chartered Manager was one of the main contributing factors which led to my recent promotion.'*
  Lloyd Ross, Programme Delivery Manager, British Nuclear Fuels

- *'I am quite sure that a part of the reason for my success in achieving my appointment was due to my Chartered Manager award which provided excellent, independent evidence that I was a high quality manager.'*
  Donaree Marshall, Head of Programme Management Office, Water Service, Belfast

- *'The whole process has been very positive, giving me confidence in my strengths as a manager but also helping me to identify the areas of my skills that I want to develop. I am delighted and proud to have the accolade of Chartered Manager.'*
  Allen Hudson, School Support Services Manager, Dudley Metropolitan County Council

- *'As we are in a time of profound change, I believe that I have, as a result of my change management skills, been able to provide leadership to my staff. Indeed, I took over three teams and carefully built an integrated team, which is beginning to perform really well. I believe that the process I went through to gain Chartered Manager status assisted me in achieving this and consequently was of considerable benefit to my organisation.'*
  George Smart, SPO and D/Head of Resettlement, HM Prison Swaleside

To find out more or to request further information please visit our website **www.managers.org.uk/cmgr** or call us on **01536 207429**.

Acknowledgements

Thanks are due to Alison Frecknall and her team at Hodder for all their support and help, to Ian Myson, Head of Product Management, Chartered Management Institute for his valuable and constructive feedback, to Ahmad M. Amarat for the excellent introduction to Jordan that he gave to my wife and me in the gap between Chapters 6 and 7 and last, but by no means least, to my partner, Linda Baguley – whose contribution was, yet again, unique.

Phil Baguley

Contents

CHAPTER 05

CHAPTER 06

CHAPTER 07

CHAPTER 08

CHAPTER 09

CHAPTER 10

CHAPTER 11

CHAPTER 12

Foreword

There has never been a greater need for better management and leadership skills in the UK. As we've seen over the past couple of years, it's all too often the case that management incompetence takes the blame for high-profile, costly and sometimes tragic failures. Put this in the context of a world dominated by changing technology and growing international competition, and every manager in this country has a responsibility for ensuring that he or she has the best possible skills to contribute to successful business performance.

So it is alarming that just one in five managers in the UK are professionally qualified. The truth is that we spend less on management development in the UK than our European competitors. Effectively this means that, if you want to develop professionally, if you want to boost your career chances, or if you just want recognition for the work you do, the onus is on you – the individual – to improve your skills. What it also means is that all of us – individual managers, employers and policy makers – need to answer difficult questions about how well equipped we are to lead in the twenty-first century. Are our standards slipping? How capable are we when it comes to meeting the skill requirements of modern business? Studies show that project management, alliance-building and communication skills are the three key 'over-arching' skills that must be mastered by the successful manager. But how many people can honestly claim they have mastery over all three?

In recent years the news has been dominated by stories focusing on breathtaking management failures. The collapse of the banking sector has been much-analysed and will continue to be discussed in the years to come. It's not just the private sector. Vast amounts of column inches have been devoted to investigations of failures across the health and social care sector, too. The spotlight has also been on management, at an individual level, as the recession deepened in the aftermath of the banking crisis, with dramatic rises in the UK's unemployment levels. Many managers are fighting an ongoing battle to control costs and survive with reduced credit and slowing demand. They are also struggling to prove their worth, to show they meet required standards now, and in the long-term.

But imagine a world where management and leadership enables top-class performance right across British businesses, the public sector and our not-for-profit organisations – where management isn't a byword for bureaucracy and failure, but plays a real role in boosting performance. The way to achieve such a realistic utopia is by developing the skills that will help you, as a manager, perform to the best of your capability. And that is why this book will help. Its aim is to provide you with practical, digestible advice that you can take straight from the pages to apply in your working environment.

Does any of this matter? Well, you wouldn't want your accounts signed off by someone lacking a financial qualification. You certainly wouldn't let an unqualified surgeon anywhere near you with a scalpel, nor would you seek an unqualified lawyer to represent your interests. Why, then, should your employer settle for management capability that is second best? It means that you need to take time out to develop your skills so that these can be evaluated and so you can stand out from the competition.

What's more, managers will play a critical role in determining how well the UK meets a wide range of challenges over the next decade. How can managers foster innovation to promote economic growth? How do they tackle the gender pay gap and the continued under-representation of women in the boardroom, as part of building truly fair, diverse organisations? Managers in all sectors will need to learn how to lead their teams through the changes we face; they will also need to be able to manage change. Above all, managers will need to grasp the nettle when it comes to managing information and knowledge. The key will rest in how they learn to manage themselves.

First-class management and leadership really can drive up both personal and corporate performance. It can boost national productivity and enhance social wellbeing. If you want to be the best manager you can be, this book is for you. In one go it will provide you with practical advice and the experience of business leaders. It is also a fascinating and enthralling read!

Ruth Spellman OBE
Chief Executive
Chartered Management Institute

01

Who is this book for?

In this, the introductory chapter of this book about leading people, you'll find out about:

- what the book sets out to do
- how it will do it, and
- what leadership skills are about.

Finally, and most importantly, it will also give you the opportunity to identify what your own individual leadership targets are.

Let's begin

So, you've decided that you want to be a leader; you may even have already begun that process of leading in your workplace. What's needed now is information about what sort of skills you need to lead, insight and guidance on how to use those skills and some perspective about this process of leading people.

Look no further.

For this is *the* book to answer all of those needs. It's a book that aims to help you, as a manager, to develop, strengthen and enhance the skills and competencies that you need to lead and direct in the workplace. Based on the Providing Direction section of the UK National Occupational Standards for Management and Leadership, its target is to enable you to become more effective when you direct the behaviour of others towards achieving the goals and objectives of your workgroup or organisation. Do this well and you'll find that the people that you work with:

- understand what is expected of them, and
- feel encouraged to meet and exceed those goals.

In short, they become *engaged* in what's happening in their workplace. The benefits of doing this are considerable: workflows will become smoother and more efficient; people will stay focused on business goals and lost time and effort will decrease. But that's not all that happens. For good leadership also generates the opportunity for people to become more comfortable and even 'happier' in the workplace. When that happens we all perform better (Table 1.1) and this leads to:

- increased productivity
- higher levels of creativity
- improved job satisfaction
- reduced staff turnover.

Table 1.1: The benefits of workplace engagement

Engaged employees:
- each take five fewer sick days/year
- raise profitability by 12 per cent and productivity by 18 per cent
- generate 43 per cent more revenue
- are 87 per cent less likely to leave

Source: UK Government Department for Business Innovation and Skills

Written for all managers who have chosen to lead others or find themselves doing that, this book will tell you:

- what leadership in the workplace is about
- what the benefits of effective workplace leadership are
- about the ways and means of effective and focused leading in the workplace
- how to successfully develop and use those ways and means, and
- how to ensure that those ways and means contribute to your personal growth and development.

Written in a clear, concise and jargon-free style with all technical terms and concepts clearly explained, the material contained in this book has a sound theoretical basis yet combines theory and practice in ways that are easily related to your experience. Rich in useful ideas, pointers to appropriate methods and helpful tools, the contents of the book are:

- practical and relevant
- accessible and easily understood
- focused on solving problems and achieving results.

Each of its chapters:

- has a title that takes the form of a question
- starts with a brief summary of its objectives and content
- finishes with a summary of its key points, a listing of the skills needed and the National Occupational Standards for Management and Leadership competences that are relevant.

These chapters are also focused on the skills that you need to be an effective leader.

Skills, what skills?

You will have already seen in both Ruth Spellman's foreword to this book and the initial part of this chapter that your ability to gain, develop and practise the skills that you need is key to the process of becoming an effective leader. However, 'skill' is a word that's often used wrongly and not always fully understood.

So, let's start your journey towards becoming an effective leader by finding out what's really meant by the word 'skill'. When I do this sort of search I always start by going to a dictionary and looking the word up. Do that and you'll find that a 'skill' is usually explained or defined as:

> 'the capability of accomplishing something with precision and certainty'

Think about this definition and you'll soon realise that you already have quite a package of skills. Some of these are basic – but nevertheless important – such as walking, talking, running, writing or jumping. When you think about it more you'll soon remember that you couldn't do these when you were born – you had to acquire these skills and then learn how to use them well. You also have a 'package' of other skills that are far less basic. These are the skills that come about when you blend together a number of different and singular skills and then use them to create a larger, more complex 'composite' skill. Being able to communicate is a good example of this. If you think about it you'll soon realise that to communicate well you need to be able to:

- listen (rather than just hear)
- speak (clearly and understandably)
- write (with precision and accuracy), and
- use your facial expressions and 'body language' to support and add to all of these.

Like everybody else, you learnt the 'how' and 'when' of singular skills when you were young. But learning the 'how' and 'when' of blending them together effectively is something different. It is, as someone once said, a skill that 'takes a lifetime to learn'.

But that's not all that you need to recognise about skills. For example, using a skill isn't a 'one-shot' event. You don't, for instance, say that someone is a skilled singer because they sing a song well *once*. Having a skill or being skilled requires the ability to be able to consistently and regularly accomplish something. So a really skilled singer will be able to sing a song well *repeatedly* – whatever the place or time. This leads us to another aspect of being skilled – the ability to develop and refine your use of a skill. Having this ability means that your use of that skill will display increasing finesse and subtlety and be responsive to the 'where and when' of its use. All of this brings us to the point where we can extend our earlier definition of a 'skill' so that it becomes:

'the capability of repeatedly accomplishing something with precision and certainty wherever and whenever needed'

Get to this point with your leadership skills and you'll find that they, and your ability to lead, are 'portable' – you'll be able to use them wherever and whenever you need to – rather than with just one sort of group of followers or in one work situation.

Leading and leadership

Later in this book you'll see that the ability to lead people is something that you develop over an extended period of time – rather than something that you're born with – a genetic or inherited trait or ability. As such it requires competence in a wide range of skills – such as communicating, planning, decision making, motivating and managing risk. Acquiring and practising these and other skills is key to your ability to carry out the process of leading people.

So let's take a quick look at how this book tells you about these skills.

It starts in Chapter 2 – What's it all about? – by exploring what is and isn't leadership. You'll read about the different sorts of leader and then take a brief look at some of the major theories about leadership. Finally, you'll arrive at the point where you'll read that the leading process is about:

- future actions
- influencing people
- establishing a direction or target for these people's collective efforts, and
- managing these activities in line with this direction or target.

One of the things that leaders often do is to create a vision of an organisation's future. To do this effectively you need somewhere to start from – a 'map' of where that organisation is now. In Chapter

3 – Who's got the map? – you'll read about how this map needs to describe the external and internal environments that surround and permeate an organisation. This chapter also looks at how your 'map' can be created, what sort of information it should contain together with some of the tools that you'll use in its creation – such as SWOT and PESTLE analyses.

Converting your vision of the future into a reality doesn't just start from a map of where you are now – it also needs a plan. In Chapter 4 – Can you see where we're going? – you'll read about the content and creation of the sort of plan that's needed – a long-term strategic business plan. Creating this sort of plan involves identifying the actions that you'll need to take and the resources needed to support those actions and then wrapping these up together in a plan that maps out a course or route that will take you from where you are now to where you want to be.

Launching a plan like this – a strategic business plan – needs care and planning. In Chapter 5 – What do we do next? – you'll look at how to do this by launching it as a project. You'll read about the ways in which that project is monitored, controlled, implemented and completed. Being a leader is a risky business – despite having a plan or project like this – and things don't always turn out the way you'd planned. In Chapter 6 – Do you take the risk? – you'll take a look at the relationship between risk and leadership. It's a chapter that starts by looking at the nature and origins of risk and then moves on to see how risk figures in, and is important to, the process of leading people. Finally, it looks at the way that you can manage your risks with its steps of identifying, analysing, evaluating and then treating risk.

Getting your communication right is a key factor in effective leadership and in Chapter 7 – Can you hear me? – you'll look at the how and when of doing just that. It's a chapter that starts by identifying the basic framework that applies to all of our communications and then looks at the strengths and weaknesses of the ways in which you communicate. Then it goes on to take a look at some of the reasons why you, as a leader, communicate and what benefits are generated by doing that effectively as well as some of the factors that can limit the effectiveness of your communications. These communications and your leading can take place in a variety of places – such as the organisation and the team. Chapter 8 – Where do you do it? – takes a look at these places and compares the characteristics and demands of each of these and the influences that they exert upon the process of your leading.

There are, of course, always more followers than leaders. In Chapter 9 – Who's following and why? – you'll read about the relationship between leader and follower and, in so doing, take a look at factors such as motivation, persuasion, influence and power – all of which are key to the process of leadership. Style, or how what is done is done, is one of the ways in which you express your individuality. As such, the influence it exerts on the quality and effectiveness of your workplace leadership is considerable. In Chapter 10 – How do you do it? – you'll read about several of the ways in which style can be described and then go on to explore the influence that style exerts upon the effectiveness of your workplace leading. In Chapter 11 – How will we do it tomorrow? – you'll briefly remind yourself about some of the key factors for the process of leadership and then move on to take a look at new and recent changes to that process.

It's always interesting to read about how other people do it and an interview with Lord Bichard (with the theme of leading people) from the CMI book *Six of the Best – Lessons in Life and Leadership* is reproduced in Chapter 12 – The Companion Interview. The links between what you've read in the book and the contents of the Providing Direction section of the NOS for Management and Leadership are identified in a section entitled National Occupational Standards.

Being a leader isn't a frozen, static, state of being and Further Information and Reading contains a list of books and websites that will give you the information, ideas and material that you'll need to carry your leadership into the future.

What's next?

By now you'll probably feel that you're ready to get on with it, to plunge into the detail of the next chapter. But there's something else that you need to do before you do that – and that's answer some questions. But these aren't questions about what you've read so far, nor are they questions about your qualifications, experience or history of leading and managing.

For these questions are about your future – as a leader.

Answering them clearly, realistically and honestly is important. Do that and you'll be able to set realistic and achievable targets for your progress on your journey to becoming a leader. It'll help you to answer these questions if you answer them in the 'here and now' – as in 'Right now, I want to _____'. Once you've done this it's worth thinking about doing a regular review or update of your answers at two-year intervals – because you, your circumstances, and the work-a-day world around you will have changed.

So, here are the questions:

1. How high do I want to fly?

This question is about your future as a leader. It's about where you want to get to and when. Answer this question realistically and honestly and you'll have taken the first step towards becoming a leader. So don't fudge your answer or kid yourself that you're ready when you're not. A good way of starting your thinking here is to take a long hard look at your current boss and his or her job. Ask yourself if you could do that job – now or at some time in the future. Identify the skill or experience gaps that are holding you back. If you honestly feel that you're ready for that job then move your focus up a notch or two – perhaps even as far as your organisation's chief executive. Get a sense of the pressures, problems and timescales that the person in that role has to deal with. Ask yourself questions like 'What does he or she do that I currently can't do?', 'Does he or she seem to be enjoying themselves?' or 'What will I have to give up to do that job?'

The outcome of all of this should be your first leadership role target and a timescale for when you aim to get there – both of which you'll write down in the appropriate part of Figure 1.1.

2. What will it cost?

If you've answered Question 1 honestly and realistically then you should be facing a couple of substantial chunks of information. These will tell you that:

- you've got knowledge and skill gaps that'll limit how far you rise
- you're going to have to give up things you enjoy doing if you want to be a leader.

Admitting to yourself that you've got these knowledge and skills gaps isn't easy. But it is realistic. As you'll see later in Table 1.2, the Providing Direction section of the National Occupational Standards for Management and Leadership lists over 40 separate skills that are needed to provide effective leadership and direction in the twenty-first century world of work. Most of these are complex composite skills that, as you saw earlier in this chapter, are formed by blending together a number of different and singular skills. Getting to any level of proficiency with this range of skills will take time, effort and sustained commitment. But if you want to lead, it's a 'must-do'. Use Table 1.2 to identify any gaps that there are in your skill portfolio and then write these down in the second box of Figure 1.1 and indicate how you're going to fill them. It's worth noting that while you're doing that you are using the skills of analysing, planning, evaluating, decision making and assessing – amongst others.

What's also a 'must-do' is finding the right work/life balance. There will be things that you do now and enjoy doing now that will have to take a back seat if you're going to be serious about being a leader. When it comes to work/family issues you're going to have to find a mix that's sustainable in the long term. All of this will mean decisions. Some of these you'll need to take on your own, others will follow the discussions that you have with your partner. All of this needs to be done with care and forethought, for as someone once observed 'Sometimes it's the smallest decisions that can change your life forever.'

Write down what you've decided and the commitment that you've made in the Question 2 part of Figure 1.1.

3. Can I keep it up?

Becoming a leader isn't, as you've probably gathered by now, an instant or even an overnight event. Even the most modest of leadership targets may take decades to achieve and you'll need to set yourself a sequence of long-term targets to reflect that reality. You'll also need, like a marathon runner, to find ways of keeping yourself going when the going gets tough and recognition and reward are thin on the ground. If you are really serious about becoming a leader then you'll need to find ways of sustaining and refreshing your physical vitality, your emotional flexibility and your intellectual reach and freshness. These need to be ways that work for you as an individual rather than run-of-the-mill or stereotypical ways of relaxing or keeping fit. Finding a way of keeping open – like an annual 'time-out' break – can reduce the danger of becoming closed and set in the ways that have worked so far. A well-used gym membership can reap dividends when it comes to your physical condition. Think about this and make a commitment to what you're going to do and then write it down in the Question 3 part of Figure 1.1.

By now you should have written down all of your answers in the appropriate part of Figure 1.1. Once you've done that read them through again – make sure that they aren't the answers that you think you ought to have written or what your boss would like you to write. They should be your personal individual answers. Make sure that they reflect *your* ambitions, *your* self-knowledge and *your* values – and then sign and date the page.

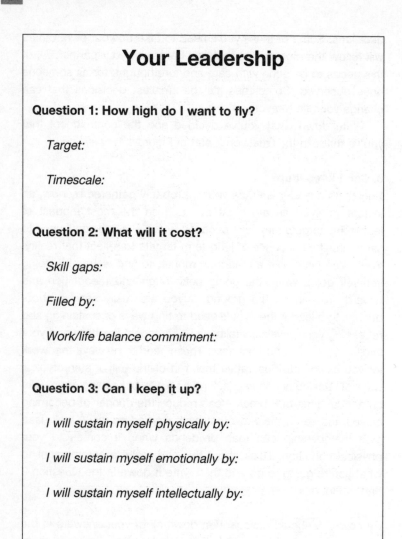

Your Leadership

Question 1: How high do I want to fly?

Target:

Timescale:

Question 2: What will it cost?

Skill gaps:

Filled by:

Work/life balance commitment:

Question 3: Can I keep it up?

I will sustain myself physically by:

I will sustain myself emotionally by:

I will sustain myself intellectually by:

Signature: Date:

Figure 1.1: Your leadership

Table 1.2: Skills listed in Providing Direction section of the National Occupational Standards for Management and Leadership B1–12

Thinking strategically	Involving others
Analysing	Negotiating
Planning	Problem solving
Risk management	Team building
Delegating	Leading by example
Networking	Obtaining and
Involving others	providing feedback
Innovating	Motivating
Consulting	Valuing and supporting
Communicating	Managing conflict
Influencing and	Coaching
persuading	Mentoring
Monitoring	Empowering
Evaluating	Learning
Setting objectives	Inspiring
Building consensus	Assessing
Decision making	Reporting
Scenario building	Reviewing
Information management	Contingency planning
Presenting information	Thinking systematically
Balancing competing needs	Bench marking
Prioritising	Following

Chapter checklist

In this chapter you've taken a look at what this book sets out to do and how it will do it. You've also taken a look at what leadership skills are about, and, most importantly, had the opportunity to identify your own leadership targets. Use the list below to check where you've got to. If you've missed something or don't understand it go back to the page given and read through it again.

- It's a book that aims to help you:
  - develop, strengthen and enhance the skills and competencies that you need to lead and direct in the workplace
  - become more effective when you direct the behaviour of others towards achieving the goals and objectives of your workgroup or organisation (page 2).
- Do this well and you'll find that the people that you work with will become *engaged* in what's happening in their workplace (page 3).
- The benefits of this happening include:
  - increased productivity
  - higher levels of creativity
  - improved job satisfaction
  - reduced staff turnover (page 3).
- Your ability to gain, develop and practise the skills that you need is key to the process of becoming an effective leader (page 4).
- A skill is *'the capability of repeatedly accomplishing something with precision and certainty wherever and whenever needed'* (page 5).
- Leadership skills are 'portable' (page 6).
- This book has twelve chapters that cover all that you need to know about becoming a leader (pages 6–8).

- You'll start your journey to becoming a leader by deciding:
  - what your leadership targets are
  - what your skill gaps are and how you're going to fill them
  - how you're going to sustain yourself on the journey to becoming an effective leader (pages 9–12).

Skills checkout

If you've attempted the exercises in this chapter you'll have used the following skills:

- analysing
- planning
- evaluating
- decision making
- reviewing, and
- assessing.

You'll also have read about the 40 or so separate skills that are needed for Units B1–12 of the Providing Direction section of the National Occupational Standards for Management and Leadership.

02

What's it all about?

In this chapter you'll start by taking a brief look at both the history – past and recent – of leading and leadership together with some of the major theories that have been developed to explain how leadership works. You'll then move on to explore why leadership gets used and what the benefits of being led are. Finally you'll take a look at three basic styles of leadership and then you'll arrive at the point where you learn more about the 'what and when' of leading.

Leading and leadership – a brief history

The words 'leader' and 'leadership' have been in common use for a long, long time. The *Oxford English Dictionary*, for example, tracks the use of 'leader' to as far back as 1300AD while 'leadership' is a relative newcomer, appearing in the early 1800s. Dig back into your history books and you'll soon find that you're reading about dynasties, kings and queens, religious movements, wars and even nations that rose, flourished and then fell in ancient days – all under the influence of one leader or another. Moses is a good example. According to the Old Testament, he was raised as royalty in ancient Egypt, became the leader of the Hebrews who were enslaved by Egypt and ultimately led over a million people out of Egypt into the surrounding wilderness – and into history. Dig further and you'll find a whole string of names associated with leading in one situation or another – history's 'A list' of fame and infamy with names like Winston Churchill, Julius Caesar, George Washington, Genghis Khan, Alexander the Great and others.

Think about all of this and you'll soon recognise that there's been a long line of leaders stretching back into the mists of prehistory and beyond. You'll also realise that, in one way or another, for good or for bad, leaders have been significant in the history of humankind.

However, leadership has only been the subject of academic studies since the middle of the twentieth century. But in the 70 or so years since then a considerable number of studies have been completed. Almost all of these have been aimed at establishing the 'how and why' of leadership. Table 2.1 lists the major theories that have been developed – ranging from the Great Man or Trait theories of the 1930s through to the almost contemporary Transformational theories. When you get to Chapter 11 – How will we do it tomorrow? – at the end of this book you'll find that it's still happening. As a result millions, if not trillions, of words have been written about leaders, leading and leadership. These have appeared in academic books and journals, business publications, general interest magazines and websites (see Further Information and Reading). What this tells you is that leaders, leading and leadership are subjects of considerable interest. You can get some confirmation of this by putting the words 'leadership' and 'leader' into Google – and generating over 100 million results and around 200 million results respectively. These compare to the 8 million results obtained for 'motherhood', 62 million for 'childhood' and 22 million for 'horoscope'. While these 'leadership' and 'leader' results are well below the 600 million and 700 million generated by 'sex' and 'money', they are, nevertheless, impressive totals – almost as high as the 250 million generated by 'football'.

Table 2.1: Leadership theories

Theory	Concepts and ideas
Great Man/Trait	Leaders are born and not bred and critical leadership traits exist and can be identified.
Charisma	Rooted in Trait theory, says that charismatic leaders display high levels of personal charm and attractiveness with significant interpersonal communication and persuasion abilities.
Behavioural	Based on the ways that leaders behave rather than what they are like.
Situational/ Contingency	No one leadership style is always right – it all depends upon the specific situation.
Transactional or Leader/Follower Exchange	Recognises importance of leader/follower relationship and focuses upon benefits of a sort of 'contract' in which rewards and recognition are traded for commitment and loyalty.
Transformational	Occurs where the leader takes a visionary position and inspires people to follow. Also looks to develop followers into leaders.

This saga of significance continues in the early twenty-first century when you find that around 85 per cent of US companies offer leadership training to their employees with research citing a per-participant cost of this training of $6,000 to $7,500 and total dollar costs in the millions.

All of this discussion and debate has, together with shifts in the world at large, led to changes in the nature of leadership. Not so long ago, the term 'leader' was an exclusive one, usually used to describe only those people (almost always men) who held positions of dominance, high power and influence. Now, in the work-a-day world of the twenty-first century, things are different. For now we live and work in a complex and changing world in which timescales from thought to action are shorter and organisations need to become leaner and flatter if they are to survive. One result of this is that the act of leading has permeated down through the organisation. It's no longer the exclusive prerogative of those who sit at the tops of our organisations. Nor is it an exclusively male domain. Now we regularly hear and read about the leadership shown by men and women who carry out many of the front line roles of our organisations – such as supervisors and team leaders.

However, not all of the news about leading and leadership has been good. The recent (2008/9) global banking crisis showed us the costs of bad leadership. By mid 2010 over 180 American banks had been closed down and, according to the Bank of England, the cost to the British economy in lost output had risen to £7.4 trillion – all of which has been caused by leadership failure. As Chris Bones, Dean of Henley Business School, writing in the *Economist* in July 2009 put it: *'But for the want of a few good men (and women) at the top of the world's financial services industry and its regulators the world's economic system was nearly destroyed.'*

But these aren't the only costs associated with leading and leadership. In Western democracies huge amounts of money are routinely spent to find out which person (or political party) will govern our country or lead us for the next few years. The 2001 UK general election, for example, cost £80 million to organise, the Canadian 2000 general election cost Can$200 million and, in the USA, the price of the answer to the question 'Who will be our President?' in 2004 was at least US$4 billion.

But, despite all of these faults, failures, difficulties and costs, history tells us that being led appears to be an experience that people want, or at least, continue to accept and, perhaps, even yearn for.

So why is this so and what are the benefits that we get from being led?

Leading and leadership – why?

Take any sort of an 'in-depth' look at leadership and its benefits and you'll soon find that the news is rather like the curate's egg – partly bad and partly good.

The bad news is that leadership remains a complex and elusive social phenomenon – despite all of the attention it has attracted. As a result, it's not yet possible to pin down a unique 'one-off' version of leadership that always works, whatever the circumstances. Despite this, the research continues – aiming to identify the true nature of leadership and thus enable its full potential.

The reasons for this are part of the good news; news that tells you that if you dig deep enough you'll find that there is some agreement about the basics of leading and leadership. This will tell you that leadership:

- is a process that involves an individual – a leader – using social influence or power
- is an on-going and continuous process rather than a 'one-shot' event
- is exerted upon groups of people rather than individuals
- includes within it the acts of leading *and* following, and, finally

- has changed and evolved to meet the demands of history.

Put simply, leadership is something that's shared, collective and social and involves the individual use of influence. It's also, as you saw earlier in this chapter, a process that humankind has continued to accept and be involved in for a long time.

There are, of course, a number of ideas as to why this has happened. One is that the process of following or being led is innate or 'hard-wired' into us while another idea argues that, as social animals, we have developed leading and following as a survival tactic – originally in order to ensure the continuing existence of our group or tribe or, more recently, to ensure the survival of our organisation or country. Other ideas include the view that the way that most businesses are structured – with a 'boss' or various layers of authority and leadership – is the most effective and efficient system for generating and maintaining productivity and profitability. Leadership has a vital role in this. The people who work in these organisations are said to need leadership for:

- direction
- motivation, and
- inspiration.

Studies show that when they get good leadership, they will, as you saw in Chapter 1:

- understand what is expected of them, and
- feel encouraged to meet and exceed their goals.

But the influence 'net' that leadership throws out reaches far beyond the boundaries of the business or organisation. For the customers, clients, suppliers, subcontractors and other agencies that provide services to that business or deal with it in other ways also need good leadership to inspire trust and confidence in the business's financial integrity, products or services and the probity of its ethics. Good leadership is also needed by the stockholders who need it to ensure a good return on their investment and by the financial markets who need it to ensure the availability of capital for the organisation when needed. But history tells us leadership isn't always good and Table 2.2 shows how, when it doesn't work, leadership can lead to some calamitous events.

Table 2.2: Political leadership – the bad news

In 2009 the expense claims made by members of the United Kingdom Parliament over several years were released into the public domain for the first time – despite attempts to prevent disclosure under Freedom of Information legislation. These showed widespread misuse of the permitted allowances and expenses claimed by Members of Parliament (MPs). All of this had taken place under the aegis of the roles of the Speaker of the House, the Prime Minister and the leaders of all the parliamentary political parties – past and present. This information was reported in all of the media. It led to widespread anger against MPs amongst the UK public and resulted in a large number of MPs resigning, being sacked or de-selected and deciding to retire. Public apologies and the repayment of expenses became common events. But, more significantly, it also led to a loss of confidence in politics that continues to this day and has given rise to pressure for political reform extending well beyond the issue of expenses.

So, given that leading and leadership are both significant and here to stay, let's take a look at the 'how' of doing them.

The how of leadership

Style, as you'll see in more detail later in this book (see Chapter 10 – How do you do it?), is about how what gets done gets done. Your leadership style will be about how you do your leading. By the end of this book you'll have explored the choices that you face and, hopefully, found the answer you need when you ask the question 'what's my personal leadership style?' With that in mind, what you need to do now is to begin to find some of the answers to another important question – 'what leadership style is best for the person, team or organisation that I'm leading?'

In order to do that you're going to take a look at three basic styles of leadership:

Authoritarian, autocratic or directive style
When you use this style you'll be telling the people you're leading what you want done and how you want it to be done. You will be very much in charge. It's a style that sometimes gets used when all the information that's needed to solve a problem is available but time is short. However, most people don't like being treated like this and, as a consequence, this style can lead to high levels of absenteeism and staff turnover. The extreme edge of this style is sometimes tainted with yelling, using demeaning language, and threats – all of which mean that, in this form, it's about bullying rather than leading.

Participative or democratic style
Using this style means that you invite one or more of the people you work with to contribute to the decision-making process. However, it's not a joint or shared decision that's taken – that's still your responsibility. The aim of this participation is to try to make sure that your decision is based on the best possible information.

It's a style that's normally used when you have part of the information, and your followers have other parts. To use this style effectively you'll need to:

- learn how to really listen to what's being said, and
- allow enough time for the discussion process.

You'll be able to read about the communication needs of leadership later in this book (see Chapter 7 – Can you hear me?). You'll also need to be aware that the more people that you involve the more time you'll need. Done well, this style can increase job satisfaction levels and help to develop skills as well as enhancing the commitment and motivation of your fellow workers. Done badly or clumsily, it's a style that can lead to frustration and de-motivation.

Delegating, empowering or 'laissez-faire' style

'Laissez-faire' is a French phrase that literally means 'let do' but is usually more broadly interpreted to mean 'let it be' or 'leave it be'. It's used here to describe a leadership style under which you'll allow the people that you work with to make the decisions. However, as the leader, you'll still be responsible for those decisions. Because of this, it's important that you keep in touch with them and monitor what is (or isn't) being achieved. Delegating leadership is at its most effective when individual team members are very experienced and skilled self-starters who are able to analyse the situation and determine what needs to be done and how to do it. Using this style means that, as the leader, you'll need to set priorities and delegate tasks. But that's not all it means – for you'll also need to be able to trust and have confidence in these people.

When you think about these styles you'll soon see that your choice of which one to use will be influenced by things like:

- how much time is available
- whether work relationships are good
- who's got the information – you, your employees, or both?
- whether your fellow workers are self-starters and have the ability to analyse the situation and determine what needs to be done and how to do it
- what sort of task you're facing – is it structured, unstructured, complicated, simple, new or done before?

Use Figure 2.1 to help you explore these alternatives in the context of solving a problem.

When you've done that what you'll see is that:

- there isn't a single 'fits-all-situations' leadership style
- the style that you use will be influenced by factors related to:
  - the situation
  - the followers
  - the relationships that you have with them.

What you'll also see is that this sort of leadership has shifted well away from the Great Man or Trait leadership to become one that's more flexible and open and with a core that's concerned with:

- future actions
- influencing people
- establishing a direction or target for these people's collective efforts
- managing these activities in line with this direction or target.

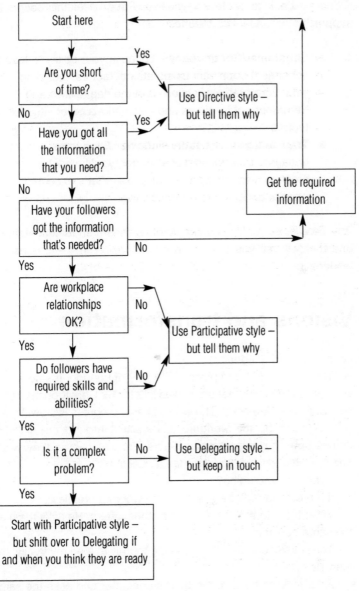

Figure 2.1: Leadership styles flow chart

If you go back to Table 2.1 you'll see that all of this seems to support these leadership theories:

- **Situational/Contingency** – because your ability to lead is contingent upon various situational factors, including what your preferred style is and the capabilities and behaviours of followers and also various other situational factors.
- **Transactional or Leader/Follower Exchange** – because, as a transactional leader, you'll work by creating clear structures that make what's expected clear and identify the rewards given.

But there is, as you'll soon see, another theory about leadership – one that will tell you about the role of vision in the process of leadership.

Visions and transformation

Let's start with a story.

The year – 1678, the place – The City of London. It's now over six months since the first stone was laid for Sir Christopher Wren's new St Paul's Cathedral. The work is hard, progress is slow. Wren, unrecognised by the workforce, is walking around the site. He comes upon a group of stonecutters. He watches as they work. Then he asks one of the workmen a question:

'What are you doing?'

'I am cutting a piece of stone,' the workman replies.

Wren turns to the second of the stonecutters. He asks the man the same question.

The answer comes – 'I am earning money to feed my family' the man says.

Finally, Wren turns to the third stonecutter and asks the same question.

This time, the answer is different.

For the man says 'I am helping Sir Christopher Wren build a magnificent cathedral to the glory of God.'

When you think about this story you'll soon realise that it's got several layers of meaning – it could be, for example, about motivation or even social inequality. But, whatever else it's about, it's also a story about having a vision; a vision that, in this case, enabled Wren to lead the team that created St Paul's, a magnificent building with a world-famous dome that still stands today.

So where should vision fit in your leadership?

The answer is simple and straightforward. This view of leadership tells you that this business of having a vision of the future is an absolute *must* if you're going to be an effective leader.

Your leadership vision can be about almost anything.

It can be about something big – such as a new product, a new way of doing things, creating an organisation that becomes a front-runner in an industry or market or serves a particular sort of customer, converting an organisation from a national 'also-ran' to an international market leader, breaking through the billion dollar turn-over barrier or creating a breakthrough in malaria or HIV treatment. It can also be about something small – such as changing the way that your team communicates or the way it handles a workload that fluctuates.

The list of potential leadership visions is, literally, endless. There's only one entry condition for this list – and that, put simply, is that your vision must be about how you perceive the future of your organisation or workplace. This idea of the vision lies at the core of what is called Transformational leadership (see Table 2.1).

Transformational leaders are different – they are unlike the transactional leaders who lead through social exchange. For they:

- stimulate and inspire those who follow them
- are capable of achieving extraordinary outcomes

- help followers to grow and develop into leaders by empowering them.

This sort of leadership is capable of stimulating change by acting in different ways. For it isn't just about overturning the old or challenging the status quo; it encourages people to explore new ways of doing things. What it is about are things like:

- having supportive relationships that have and use open and clear lines of communication
- encouraging the sharing of ideas and recognising contributions
- being based on a clear vision that has been articulated to followers and is shared by them.

What vision?

The where and when of your vision's arrival aren't important. It can arrive unbidden, spring into your mind in the shower one morning or during your evening commute home or you can create it under more formal circumstances – such as in a strategy seminar or at a business meeting.

But once your vision has arrived – what do you do with it?

If you're really going to be a transformational leader then you're going to have to do two things. The first of these is to hold on to your vision. As management guru Peter Senge tells us, you'll have to have *'the capacity to hold a shared picture of the future we seek to create'*. You'll notice there's a *'we'* in that quote – as in *'we seek to create'*. For therein lies the key to the second thing that you have to do. For you have to share that vision or picture of the future with others. As a transformational leader you'll need to do that from the beginning. When you do that you'll start the process of empowering and inspiring those you work with. Do it well and they'll begin to see themselves:

- *inside*, rather than outside, the vision, and
- seeing the future it describes as *their* future.

To get to this point your vision has to be uplifting, encouraging experimentation and innovation and capable of overturning the 'status quo'.

When people buy into a vision like this it energises and inspires them. This happens because the vision gives them a glimpse of a 'might-be/could-be' future. That glimpse acts as a catalyst or change agent that intensifies and expands both their efforts and their outcomes or effects.

Communicating the vision

You've already seen that, as a transformational leader, you have to be able to share that vision with the people who'll be directly involved in its implementation.

Get this right and your vision will enter the 'vision action zone'.

This is where your vision will move away from being 'yet-to-be-actioned' by a sequence of actions that looks like this:

Vision → Plan → Actions → Outcome

Doing all of this takes effort and people – and people, as you'll see later in this book, are key to the process. Get this sharing right and you'll find that something great will happen – they'll take your vision 'on board' as their own and when that happens they will contribute to your vision, making it even more challenging and attractive.

The way that you'll achieve this is really quite simple – you'll get them to talk about that vision. You can do this in any one of a number of ways – such as one-on-one talks, round table discussions, 'town-hall' meetings, conference calls, team meetings, board meetings, staff meetings, company dinners or outings, off-sites, video and audio tapes, blogs, tweets, discussion papers or newsletters. Any one or more of these will work – it's really a question of choosing the ones that are appropriate. But, whatever your choice might be, remember that it has to have a single objective: to get people talking about 'the vision'.

It's important to remember that you also need to share your vision with those people who aren't directly involved in the 'vision action zone'. These, the 'outside' stakeholders, will include people in other teams or departments, suppliers, customers and clients. If you've got a really big vision you might even want to include the Board, investors, the media, even the government. Why do you need to do this?

The answer is, again, quite simple. For when the 'outside' world actively participates in the future of your team or department or company, what happens then is that they too buy into your vision and when that happens all sorts of things that were once difficult become easy.

Moving forward

But if sharing the vision is all that you do it isn't going to get you very far. To move forward – through the 'vision action zone' from vision to outcome – you're going to need to enable others to do things. To do that you're going to have to follow a sequence that goes something like this:

- Develop a strategic plan for the achievement of your vision.
- Action that plan and so translate your vision into actions.
- Realise the vision through small planned steps and small successes.
- Be confident, decisive and optimistic about your vision through all of these steps.

You'll be able to read about the how, why and when of the steps in this sequence in the following chapters of this book. This process starts with the next chapter that will tell you about your first step – that of creating the 'map' for the journey that'll take you from where it is now to become an outcome. But before you start that chapter why not check out your leadership awareness in Figure 2.2 (see page 35).

Chapter checklist

In this chapter you've taken a look at the core issues of leading and leadership.

Use the list below to check where you've got to. If you've missed something or don't understand it go back to the page given and read through it again.

- Leadership has been around for a long time (page 17).
- There are a number of theories about how leadership works (page 18).
- Leadership doesn't always succeed (pages 20 and 23).
- Leadership remains a complex and elusive social phenomenon (page 21).
- Leadership is shared, collective and social and involves the individual use of influence (page 22).
- Good leadership provides:
  - direction
  - motivation, and
  - inspiration (page 22).
- Leadership has a field of influence that extends beyond the boundaries of the business or organisation (page 22).
- The three basic styles of leadership are:
  - authoritarian
  - participative, and
  - laissez-faire (pages 24–25).

- The leadership style that you use will depend upon a number of factors such as:
  - how much time is available
  - quality of work relationships
  - skill levels
  - task complexity, and
  - quality and amount of information available (page 26).
- Your use of situational leadership will depend upon situational factors and your use of transactional leadership will need you to create clear reward/effort structures (page 28).
- Transformational leadership starts from a personal vision and is capable of extraordinary outcomes (page 29)
- Your vision can be about anything (page 29).
- People will take that vision on board when they talk about it (page 31).
- To move that vision forward you'll need to:
  - develop a strategic plan for the achievement of your vision
  - action that plan and so translate your vision into actions
  - realise the vision through small planned steps and small successes
  - be confident, decisive and optimistic about your vision through all of these steps (page 32).

Under each of the headings below circle the number that's nearest to the way that you feel that you lead or feel about leading. Then add up your total and go to the Scoring section below.

I always lead my team the same way	1 2 3 4 5 6 7	I try to work out which way is best for this team
I tell people what I think	1 2 3 4 5 6 7	I listen when people talk and they listen when I talk
These things usually sort themselves out	1 2 3 4 5 6 7	People have to know what to do, when and how to do it
We pay them, isn't that enough?	1 2 3 4 5 6 7	I see my team as creative problem solvers
I let problems solve themselves	1 2 3 4 5 6 7	I decide quickly and with the information that we've got

Scoring

Total

5–15   You seem to be having problems!

15–25   Well done – now use your low scores to identify where you need to be more leadership aware

25–35   Congratulations! Now you need to look at the lows in your marking and see if you can bring them up. You also need to remember that you and the world around you are constantly changing and make sure that you and your leadership style don't drift out of touch with reality.

Figure 2.2: How's your leadership awareness?

Skills checkout

If you've thought about using or have actually used Figures 2.1 and 2.2 then you'll have used the following skills:

analysing	planning
evaluating	setting objectives
decision making	reviewing
assessing	

You'll also have read about using the skills of involving others, communicating, influencing and persuading, building consensus, motivating and learning. All of these are needed for Units B1–12 of the Providing Direction section of the National Occupational Standards for Management and Leadership.

03

Who's got the map?

Shifting your vision from 'might-be' to 'actual' is a process that starts with the act of creating a 'map' of where you are now. This 'map' will describe the external and internal environments that surround, influence and infiltrate your workplace and organisation. This chapter looks at how that 'map' can be created and what sort of information it should contain together with some of the tools that get used in its creation – such as SWOT and PESTLE analyses.

Maps – why and when?

If you're like me, you'll think that maps – paper, geographical ones, that is – are fascinating things. They give you a flat, foldable, portable, two-dimensional, geometrically accurate, drawn-to-scale picture of the three-dimensional real world. It's a picture that's rich in information – it uses hundreds of symbols to represent what's actually on the ground and lines to show the contours of the land. But, despite all this information, there's really only one purpose that I put my maps to – to plan and navigate my journeys.

And that is what you want a map for. If your journey to convert your vision from 'hoped-for' to 'tangible' is going to be successful, you'll need a map. You'll need it to:

- find out what's ahead
- plan your journey
- navigate your way to success.

But the map that you're going to need on this journey will be different from the geographical maps that you're used to. For, instead of showing the roads, trails and pathways that you walk or drive along, it'll have to show other sorts of tracks and trails – the ones that criss-cross your workplace. These will carry information, materials and products rather than cars, buses trains or people. But that's not all that your map will need to show. For your workplace operates within a larger, more complex, environment. In this there is a wide spectrum of external factors and influences, all of which you'll need to take into account and make allowances for in your vision's journey from 'hoped-for' to 'tangible'.

In this chapter you'll start by looking at the 'micro' environment – the day-by-day or week-by-week operations that go on inside your organisation and workplace. Then you'll move on to look at its 'macro' environment – the larger scale arena in which internal and external factors influence your organisation. In both of these, you'll be looking at the nature and potential of what goes on and seeing how you can find out about these can help or hinder your vision.

So, let's begin our map making.

Day by day, week by week

The sorts of things that go on in organisations and workplaces on a day-by-day or week-by-week basis are usually called 'operations'. These, put simply, are about the way things get done within that organisation or workplace. For almost all organisations, these operations involve the production of goods or services. In order to do this – carry out their operations – these organisations need to acquire, get hold of or buy resources and then convert these into products of one sort or another. But that's not all that happens – for these products then have to be distributed to their customers who then use the products or sell them on.

One way of describing all of this is to say that all organisations, at their core and whatever they produce, are systems or mechanisms for conversion or transformation (see Figure 3.1).

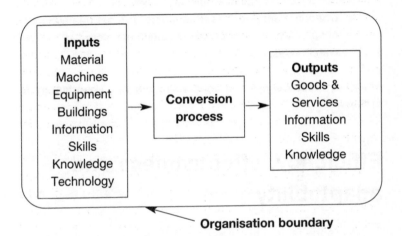

Inputs
Material
Machines
Equipment
Buildings
Information
Skills
Knowledge
Technology

Conversion process

Outputs
Goods & Services
Information
Skills
Knowledge

Organisation boundary

Figure 3.1: The conversion process

But the stuff that gets converted or transformed isn't always solid stuff like the metals and plastics that cars, for example, get made from. These 'inputs' can also be far less tangible – like the information and knowledge that's converted into a book and the utilities (gas and electricity) that get used in the conversion process.

When you think about it you'll soon realise that there's an enormous variety of inputs and outputs in the organisations around you. One useful way of looking at all this variety is to label these organisations according to what they do. When you do this it tells you that they:

- **manufacture** – as when you physically create something such as a car, tv set or a refrigerator, or
- **transport** – as when you move something from one place to another as in an airline, taxi service, bus service or a road haulier, or
- **supply** – as when a change of ownership of goods occurs as in retail or wholesale outlets, or
- **provide a service** – as when customers get treated in hospital wards or materials or goods get stored in warehouses.

Efficiency, effectiveness and adaptability are very important in all of these.

Efficiency, effectiveness and adaptability

These are the factors that you'll use to measure and monitor the performance of your operations unit. But that's not the only use that you'll put them to. For the drive to increase that performance is an ever-present 'must' in the twenty-first century and without these factors you'll be like a ship without a compass or, to put it in more modern day terms, without a GPS.

So, let's take a look at them.

Efficiency

In its simplest form, efficiency is expressed as a ratio. This is a ratio that compares the outputs of your operations to the inputs that you used to create them. Apply this idea to your car and you'll find its efficiency being measured by the ratio of miles driven to gallons or litres of petrol, gasoline or diesel used. However, things are generally more complicated than this in the work-a-day world and, as a result, you'll need to use different sorts of ratios. Take a look at Table 3.1 below and you'll see some examples.

But, before you do that, remember that these and the many other efficiency measures or ratios that exist:

- are only concerned with resource utilisation
- are **not** concerned with whether the unit's output is relevant and available when and where required.

Effectiveness

When you think about your unit's operations you'll soon realise that efficiency, important as it is, isn't the only factor that influences its survival.

Take an over-arching view of what's happening there and you'll soon see that it's just as important that your unit provides the right service and does that at the right place and time. Do this and you'll soon find the benefits of being effective. Table 3.1 below illustrates the change that happens when you start to factor effectiveness into your operations.

Table 3.1: Efficiency and effectiveness

	Efficiency ratios	Effectiveness ratios
Shop assistant	customers served/hour	average sale/customer
Hotel clerk	minutes/telephone call	% calls leading to a booking
Newspaper reporter	reporter hours/story	% stories published in paper
Purchasing manager	cost/purchased unit	% stock outs/stock turn

When you think about this shift from efficiency to effectiveness you'll soon realise that, helpful as it is, it also brings with it the potential for problems. If, for example, your workplace uses an efficiency metric to monitor its performance then the shift to an effectiveness metric based on customer needs isn't going to look good. But, if your vision is about creating that shift, you'll have already taken this into account. For, as you saw in Chapter 2, you'll have already shared that vision with the people who operate both inside and outside the 'vision action zone'.

Adaptability

It's been observed that there are many natural living systems that possess the ability to reach a desired end point or outcome when starting from different points in the environment and using different resources. When you apply this idea – which is about open systems and called *equifinality* – to businesses it suggests that organisations may establish similar competitive advantages based on substantially different competencies. That is that similar results may be achieved from different starting points and in many different ways.

There are a number of good things about this. But the two most important ones are, firstly, that it echoes something that you read in Chapter 2 – when you saw that there isn't a single 'fits-all-situations' leadership style – and, secondly, that it's this characteristic that leads to what are often called the 'legends' of good customer service. These include the hotels that can remember and answer your special idiosyncratic needs and the airlines that hold flights open until the last minute because of bad traffic or heavy weather on the road from town. Adaptable organisations get to where they are by:

- empowering their employees

- creating and refining flexible operating systems
- placing customer needs ahead of their own.

All of these are among the outcomes of effective leadership.

Moving forward

At the end of the last chapter you read about the things that you needed to do to move forward through the 'vision action zone' from vision to outcome. You saw that you're going to have to go through a sequence of small planned steps and small successes.

Improving your operations performance is key to making that happen.

To do that you'll need to be:

- constantly seeking new ways to improve your unit's performance
- always making sure that these new ways reach out towards and support your vision of your unit's future.

You'll also need to be sure that the objectives that you aim for are:

- **DUMB** – as in **D**oable, **U**nderstandable, **M**anageable and **B**eneficial, and
- **SMART** – as in **S**pecific and **S**imple, **M**easurable and **M**eaningful, **A**ttainable and **A**ppropriate, **R**ealistic and **R**elevant as well as **T**imebased and **T**angible.

When you aim for those objectives you'll use the process that's illustrated in Figure 3.2.

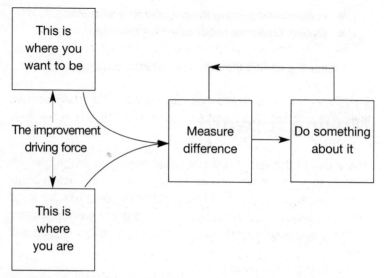

Figure 3.2: The improvement driving force

One of the ways by which you can identify targets for your improved performance involves the process of benchmarking.

Benchmarking

The word 'benchmark' was first used by surveyors – it's a mark cut into suitable rock surface to indicate a level. Nowadays, the process of generating a benchmark – or benchmarking – is different. It's the process whereby you can compare the performance of your organisation to the best performance for the industry you're in or the best performance from other industries. These are called benchmarks and they're about performance metrics such as quality, productivity, sales/m², etc.

This process of benchmarking is a continuous one with the objectives of:

- understanding and evaluating the current position of an organisation or workplace in relation to 'best practice'
- identifying ways and means of performance improvement.

Doing this involves looking outward to examine how others achieve their performance levels and to understand the processes they use. It involves four key steps:

1. Getting to know and understand your existing processes in detail.
2. Analysing the processes of others – by developing benchmarking partners or using trade associations.
3. Comparing your performance with others and generating a benchmark for performance improvement.
4. Implementing the steps necessary to close the performance gap.

The resultant benchmarks or targets for performance improvement can be:

- strategic – about core competencies, new products and services
- about key products and services – usually involves use of benchmarking partners from the same sector or industry but can also use trade associations
- about critical processes and operations – uses benchmarking partners that are best practice organisations and undertake similar operations and processes or deliver similar services.

The benchmarking partners that you use can be internal – such as business units in different countries or subsidiaries, or external – such as organisations that use similar processes to produce different products. The advantages of using internal partners include:

- easier access to confidential performance data
- data is expressed or measured in the same way
- easier communication
- less time and resources needed
- practices transfer is often easy in the same organisation.

However, real innovation may be lacking and the consensus is that 'best in class' performance is more likely to be found through external benchmarking.

Now you're ready to move on – to take a look at your organisation's 'macro' environment.

The bigger picture

Your organisation or workgroup doesn't exist on its own. Whatever its outcomes or products are, it'll always operate in and be a part of a much larger arena. When you look at that arena or environment you'll soon find it contains a considerable number of other organisations or groups. All of these exert influence upon your organisation and upon each other. Figure 3.3 shows some of the major organisations or groups that interact with a typical organisation.

If you're looking at a small unit – such as a team within a department – then the general arrangement of this picture will be the same except that many of the 'satellites' will change – to be other teams or workgroups or departments.

It's very important that you develop and maintain an awareness of these influences on your vision's journey from 'hoped-for' to 'tangible'. You've already seen, for example (in Chapter 2 – What's it all about?), that you need to take account of these 'outside' stakeholders in the very earliest stages of your vision's journey. One aspect of the influence exerted by this external environment is the need for your workplace or organisation to comply with the law

Figure 3.3: The environment

in its various forms. This legal influence is often exerted in specific areas – such as health and safety, employment, finance, accounting and company law. Apart from making sure that your organisation complies with these laws you'll also have to take into account the specific regulations and ethical frameworks that'll exist for the industry that your organisation operates in. As a leader you'll need to be aware of all of these – a time consuming but necessary task. But this awareness shouldn't just tell you about the size or significance of these influences; it should also enable you to assess their nature and 'polarity'.

Sounds difficult or complicated? Well, it isn't because there are tools that you can use to help you do this.

PESTLE and SWOT

When you carry out PESTLE and SWOT analyses you're doing that because you need to find out where your organisation is. Both of these are usually described as 'strategic planning tools'. The main difference between them – apart from their acronymic titles – is that PESTLE looks outward into the environment that surrounds your organisation or workgroup whereas SWOT looks inward at the organisation or workgroup itself.

But what do these acronyms stand for? Here's the answer:

- **PESTLE** analysis looks at the **P**olitical, **E**conomic, **S**ocial, **T**echnological, **L**egal and **E**nvironmental aspects of the environment that your organisation or workgroup operates in.
- **SWOT** analysis looks at the **S**trengths, **W**eaknesses, **O**pportunities and **T**hreats of that organisation or workgroup.

The usual sequence is that you do your PESTLE analysis first and then use its results to add additional focus to the SWOT analysis of your organisation or workgroup's internal strengths and weaknesses.

So let's take a look at how you do that.

PESTLE analysis

You've already seen that a PESTLE analysis examines and describes the political, economic, social, technological, legal and environmental factors and influences that exist within the environment in which your organisation or workgroup operates. The history of this analysis is obscure but seems to have its roots in a more basic version – ETPS (Economic, Technical, Political and

Social) – that was developed in the late 1960s. PESTLE has recently been extended to STEEPLED, which now includes education and demographic factors. It's often seen as a useful strategic tool that helps you to understand such changes as market growth or decline, business position, potential and direction for operations.

So, let's look at each of these factors in more detail.

Political

This relates to what is happening politically in the environment in which you operate and includes areas such as tax policy, trade restrictions, tariffs and political stability. In some environments it may also include goods and services that the current government does or doesn't want to be provided. Don't forget that governments also have great influence on the health, education, and infrastructure of a nation.

Economic

This is about what's happening to the economy. Specifics will include economic growth or the lack of it, interest rates, currency exchange rates, inflation or deflation rate, wage or salary rates, minimum wage, working hours, unemployment, ease of access to credit, retail price and cost of living index changes.

Social

This is about what's happening socially in the markets that you operate in – such as immigration rates from other countries and cultures, changes in cultural norms, life experience expectations, health consciousness, population growth rate, age distribution, career attitudes and emphasis on safety.

Technology

Technology, as you know, is changing and developing all of the time. Mobile phone technology, email, web 2.0, blogs, social networking websites and VOIP systems are all examples of not only what can happen but also how quickly it can happen. These and those technological developments yet to come will impact upon your products or services. New technologies can lead to barriers to entry in given markets and changes to financial decisions about levels of R&D investment, use of out- and in-sourcing and minimum production levels. Shifts in the technology that you use to generate your products or service your clients will affect costs, quality and innovation levels.

Legal

This will include existing legislation – such as discrimination law, consumer law, antitrust law, employment law and health and safety law – and new or potential laws together with any proposed or potential changes and additions to those laws. All of these can have a significant effect upon how your organisation or workgroup company operates, what its costs are, and what the demand is for its products.

Environmental

Environmental factors are becoming increasingly significant in the work-a-day worlds of the twenty-first century. There's an increasing awareness of climate change and its implications; implications that can affect how your organisation or workplace operates and the products they offer. Climate and climate change are, for example, affecting industries such as tourism, farming, and insurance and creating new markets as well as destroying existing ones.

PESTLE – How to do it

The steps that you need to take when you're doing a PESTLE analysis are really quite straightforward and obvious. There are, in the basic form of this analysis, ten in total:

1. Decide how you're going to collect the information that you need.
2. Agree who's going to do the collecting – generally teams work better than individuals.
3. Identify and get access to appropriate sources of information.
4. Gather and record the information – templates can be useful here for both exploring and recording the information (see Table 3.2 for a sample checklist and Figure 3.4 for a simple template).
5. Analyse the findings – you'll find it useful to grade the factors identified in terms of timescale and significance.
6. Identify the most important issues – pick out those with the shortest timescale and/or highest significance.
7. Identify your options for action.
8. Write a report – make sure there's an executive summary at the front.
9. Distribute the report.
10. Decide which trends you're going to monitor on an ongoing basis.

Table 3.2: Sample checklist

Category: Social
Lifestyle changes and trends
Demographics
Consumer buying patterns
Fashion
Role models
Consumer attitudes and buying patterns
Ethnic factors
Religious factors
Ethical issues

Category	Factors
Political	
Economical	
Social	
Technology	
Legal	
Environmental	

Figure 3.4: PESTLE analysis

SWOT analysis

This is the tool that you'll use to evaluate the Strengths, Weaknesses, Opportunities, and Threats involved in your project to shift your vision from 'hoped-for' to 'complete'. It's a simple technique that was developed in the late 1960s by Albert Humphrey, an American management consultant and chemical engineer who specialised in organisational management and cultural change. SWOT analysis can be used in an enormous variety of situations: at corporate or organisational level, in a business unit or at operations level, in profit making or non-profit-making organisations and by an individual or an organisation.

In its simplest form SWOT analysis can be used in any decision-making situation in which a desired outcome or objective has been identified.

The aim of the analysis is to identify the key factors that influence and are important to the achievement of that outcome or objective. These, of course, will be particular to the work unit, organisation or individual involved. The analysis aims to identify information 'bits' that are key to the defined objective and then group these into one of two main categories:

- **Internal factors:** These are *strengths* and *weaknesses* of the organisation, work unit or individual.
- **External factors:** The *opportunities* and *threats* presented by the environment that's external to the organisation, workgroup or individual.

You can, and probably will, use the outcomes of your PESTLE analysis to help identify some of these external factors. Take a look at Table 3.3 for another definition of the factors that go to make up a SWOT analysis.

Table 3.3: SWOT factors

> **Strengths:** attributes that will help you to achieve the objective
>
> **Weaknesses:** attributes that hinder the achievement of the objective
>
> **Opportunities:** external conditions that will help you to achieve the objective
>
> **Threats:** external conditions that could do damage to the objective

SWOT – how to do it

Carrying out a SWOT analysis involves you in systematically identifying your business unit or organisation's strengths or strong points and weaknesses together with the opportunities and threats that it's currently facing. It's usually carried out by a group but can be a solo effort. It does, however, need to be done systematically and objectively. There's little point in either overrating or underrating any of the issues involved – unless, of course, you include 'management lack of perspective' as a weakness in your analysis! The results of your analysis should clearly and unambiguously identify all of the relevant issues and will provide you with all the information you need. Table 3.4 contains an example of the outcome of a SWOT analysis and Table 3.5 identifies the steps that you'll need to take in doing your SWOT analysis.

Table 3.4: Strengths, Weaknesses, Opportunities and Threats

A small manufacturing business generated the following SWOT analysis:

Strengths
- able to respond very quickly – no red tape, no need for higher management approval
- current workloads mean able to devote time to customers and thus provide really good customer care
- strong local reputation
- low overheads
- can offer good value to customers
- key skilled personnel who are flexible and open to new technologies

Weaknesses
- some staff have limited skills in some areas
- no national market presence or reputation
- vulnerable to key staff being sick, leaving, etc.
- cash flow can be unreliable

Opportunities
- business sector is expanding
- local council wants to encourage local businesses with work where possible
- competitors may be slow to respond to and adopt new technologies

Threats
- will developments in technology take us beyond our ability to adapt?
- a small change in focus of a large competitor might wipe out any market position that we have.

Table 3.5: SWOT analysis – the key steps

The steps involved in completing a SWOT analysis are very similar to those that you used in the PESTLE analysis. It is, nevertheless, essential that you are systematic and objective in the way that you carry out these steps.

1. Decide how and by whom the information is to be collected.
2. Identify and get access to sources of information.
3. Gather the information.
4. Assess and collate the information under the appropriate heading.
5. Rate the issues identified in terms of:
   - urgency of response required, and
   - importance.
6. Identify your action options.
7. Decide which actions are a priority.
8. Record and distribute information and findings in a report.

Chapter checklist

In this chapter you've taken a look at the ways and means of describing the external and internal environments that surround and permeate your workplace and organisation. Use the list below to check where you've got to. If you've missed something or don't understand it go back to the page given and read through it again.

- The day-by-day operations of your organisation or workplace are about converting resources into products or services (page 38).
- Your conversion process can be about: manufacture, or transport, or supply, or providing a service (page 40).

- Efficiency, effectiveness and adaptability are very important in all of these (page 40).
- Efficiency = Output/Input (page 40).
- Effectiveness happens when your unit provides the *right* service at the *right* place and time (page 41).
- Adaptability happens when you:
  - empower the people who work with you
  - create and refine flexible operating systems
  - place customer needs ahead of your own (page 42).
- The operating objectives that you aim for should be:
  - **DUMB** as in **D**oable, **U**nderstandable, **M**anageable and **B**eneficial,
  - **SMART** as in **S**pecific and **S**imple, **M**easurable and **M**eaningful, **A**ttainable and **A**ppropriate, **R**ealistic and **R**elevant as well as **T**imebased and **T**angible (page 43).
- Benchmarking is a way of identifying your targets for performance improvement page 44).
- Your organisation or work group operates in a much larger arena that contains a considerable number of other organisations or groups, all of which exert an influence upon your organisation and upon each other (page 46).
- You can assess these influences by doing **PESTLE** and **SWOT** analyses (page 48).
- A **PESTLE** analysis looks outward into the environment that surround your organisation or workgroup (page 48).
- A **SWOT** analysis looks inward at the organisation or workgroup itself (page 48).
- Do your **PESTLE** analysis first and then use its results to add additional focus to your **SWOT** analysis (page 48).
- A **PESTLE** analysis looks at the **P**olitical, **E**conomic, **S**ocial, **T**echnological, **L**egal and **E**nvironmental aspects of the environment that your organisation or work group operates in (pages 48–52).

- A **SWOT** analysis looks at the Strengths, Weaknesses, Opportunities and Threats of that organisation or workgroup (pages 53–56).
- Both of these must be carried out in ways that are systematic and objective.

Skills checkout

Doing, rather than just reading about, the things that you've been reading about in this chapter will be quite a demanding task. It'll need you to continue to develop, refine and expand your individual 'bundle' of skills.

If you think about what you've read you'll soon realise that these will include skills such as:

analysing	risk assessment
planning	networking
evaluating	involving others
decision making	communicating
reviewing	managing information
assessing	scenario building
setting objectives	measuring and monitoring
presenting information	thinking strategically
valuing and supporting others	motivating
monitoring	risk management
reporting	

You'll also have noticed the need to be able to set objectives, influence, persuade and build a consensus. All of these are needed for Units B1, B2 and B8 of the Providing Direction section of the National Occupational Standards for Management and Leadership.

04

Can you see where we're going?

This chapter is about the why and how of creating a long-term strategic business plan – the sort of plan that you'll need if you're going to convert your vision into a reality. Creating a plan like this involves identifying the actions that you'll need to take and the resources needed to support those actions and then wrapping these up together in a plan that maps out a course to bring you from where you are now to where you want to be.

Plans and planning

The actions of creating, setting up and implementing a plan are common enough in the business world of the twenty-first century. Like your vision of your organisation's future, these plans can be about almost anything – sales, marketing, production, finance, publishing, operations etc. But, whatever their subject might be, they all have one thing in common – that is they are all attempts to shape and control the future. In order to do that they all have a specific and defined outcome or objective and an allied set of linked intended actions. These actions are, of course, aimed at achieving that outcome.

Most of these plans are focused towards outcomes that are, for one reason or another, important. Because of this they get written down, recorded and stored. Doing this helps with the management and control of your plan as well as making it accessible. But that isn't all that's needed – there's lots of evidence that tells us that the absence of a 'well-laid' plan can have serious negative effects. If you try, for example, to climb Everest without a plan, you'll soon run out of food or oxygen or get stranded without the porters and guides that your expedition needs. But this can't be just any old 'back of an envelope' plan – it needs to be a plan that looks carefully and thoroughly at the needs of all the actions required for its completion. Fail to do that and you're planning for failure – not success.

This act of creating a plan can be as simple as writing a straightforward list of actions or as complex as inputting several thousand linked actions into a sophisticated computer program. Once completed, it should give you an action plan or sequence of actions that you can then start to implement.

Sounds simple, doesn't it?

But it isn't – for effective planning takes the ability to link together multiple and diverse strings of actions in ways that ensure that they all get done at the 'right' time. Doing this and doing it well takes real skill and ability. There's much more about the detail of doing this in some of the books listed in Further Information and Reading at the end of the book.

But when you've done it you'll find that you have a real plan or road map. That is what you need to convert your vision into a reality – a long-term strategic business plan.

Long or short view?

The idea of having a strategy or strategic plan has been around for a long time. But by the mid-twentieth century the idea of strategy had outgrown its limited military origins and was in widespread use in business firms and corporations. This 'application shift' has persisted. As a result, when you now put the phrase 'business strategy' in the search box of your favourite online bookseller's website you'll probably come up with over 46,000 books. As a result, it won't do any harm if we try to introduce some clarity into your use of this overworked word and in so doing take a look at what the word 'strategy' really means in the twenty-first century for you on your road to implementing your leadership vision.

But before you get much further into that there are three things that you need to recognise:

1. You'll be looking at strategy in the context of your organisation or workplace – rather than battle fields or campaigns.
2. You'll be using a top-down approach – rather than the operations led bottom-up approach that you used in the previous chapter.
3. Your strategy will be about the long term – but it will also have significant and sometimes immediate implications in the short term.

Take a look at Figure 4.1 and you'll start to get a more detailed idea of what's happening here.

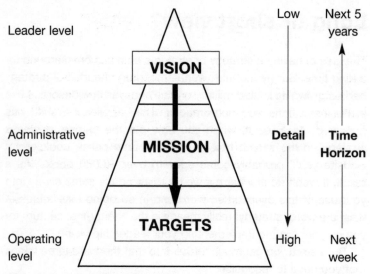

Figure 4.1: From vision to targets

So, where do you go from here?

If you dig into the mountains of material that have been written about business strategy, you'll find, at its core, some basic facts. These will tell you that strategy is about:

- direction – where *is* the business going?
- time scale – undoubtedly long term but with medium- and short-term implications
- markets – which ones and why?
- advantage – what's your advantage?
- resources – what do you need to make sure that you'll win?
- externals – what environmental and stakeholder pressures and influences are about?

So, let's bring them together.

Your strategic plan – why?

As you've already see, there's been a lot of talk about strategic planning since it moved over into the business arena. As a result, it's become *the* popular, if not *the* 'fashionable' thing to do. But if you're a small business owner you'll probably say that sort of thing is for the 'big guys' and, anyway, with all that's happening these days, you don't have time. Similarly, if you're in charge of a small workgroup or section in a large company, you'll probably argue that this sort of stuff is for the division heads.

So, why do you need a strategic plan and what are its benefits? Here are some of the answers:

1. A strategic plan sets specific goals and objectives – these will identify a clear path to your success.
2. A strategic plan will help you focus on the important things – like which activities are the most profitable and should get first call on scarce resources.
3. Get yourself a strategic plan and you'll find that you've got a road map – one that'll tell you the detail of your vision's route from idea to reality and how you're going to get there.
4. Share your plan with your fellow workers and you'll find that it gives them a better understanding of the workgroup's direction and goals. When that happens they'll become engaged, feel part of the team and take ownership in the success of the plan.
5. Preparing your plan will tell you about your organisation's:
   - strengths and weaknesses
   - opportunities and threats.
   Knowing about these will tell you about:
   - the areas in which you need help
   - when to go with your strengths

    - the threats you need to guard against
    - the opportunities you need to grasp.

But, despite all of these benefits, there's one thing that a strategic plan won't do – it won't make you immune to what the famous English playwright William Shakespeare called the 'slings and arrows of outrageous fortune'. But when these 'yet-to-be-seen' or 'yet-to-happen' threats or catastrophes of outrageous fortune do arrive, having a strategic plan will mean that you'll be able to cope well. It will also save you time and money as well as improving your resource utilisation.

Remember that your strategic plan doesn't have to be a lengthy document or involve a great deal of expense or time. But it does need to be well thought out and, as you'll see in the next section, well timed.

But if you're still not sure about the value of a strategic plan for your organisation or workplace use the questionnaire in Figure 4.2.

Your strategic plan – when?

There are no set 'must-do' rules about when you do your strategic planning. It's one of those issues that you're going to have to make your own mind up about. But there are a couple of issues that you'll do well to bear in mind when you're doing that. These are:

- what sort of an organisation you're in
- what's happening in that organisation.

Let's take a look at these separately and in more detail.

Statement	Yes	Maybe	No
We have a clear vision of what we want to achieve.			
There is good agreement about the vision.			
We reguarly discuss our strengths and weaknesses and the opportunities and threats in the environment.			
We have expressed our vision in terms of clear goals and objectives.			
We have a mission statement that says what we do, who we do it for and why it is important.			
Prioritisation – of what we must do, what we should do and what we would like to do – is good.			
We use good performance metrics.			
We work in a relatively stable environment.			
There have been no major changes in the past year.			
Total **Points** **Points total =**			
Score answers as follows: Yes = 1 Maybe = 2 No = 3			
If your overall total is 19 or more, then you're ready for strategic planning. If it's between 15 and 18, then your organisation probably would benefit from a strategic planning process. Under 10, then there is no urgency but you should do a review within three years.			

Figure 4.2: Strategic planning questionnaire

What sort of organisation?

Size is a crucial element here. For example, a large complex organisation with several divisions and an extensive catalogue of products will probably have a department or section that's dedicated to the creation, monitoring and maintenance of its strategic plan. The planning horizon of this plan will be three to five years but progress towards its completion will be audited annually – usually in time for the results to be integrated into the organisation's financial plan for the coming year. Medium–small organisations will work to a similar timeline but will use line staff to create and maintain their strategic plans.

But when you come to look at small or non-profit-making organisations you'll soon see that things are different. Small organisations, for example, rarely have the in-house resources that are needed to create a strategic plan. Similarly, non-profit organisations often suffer from the same limitation with the additional complication of having a lot of part-time or voluntary employees. In both of these situations, the use of a part-time consultant can often help.

What's happening in your organisation?

All of the above can change in response to what's happening in your organisation and its immediate external environment. For example, an organisation whose products and services exist in a volatile and rapidly changing marketplace will be under some pressure to carry out its strategic planning fully once or even twice a year. However, an organisation that's serving a fairly stable marketplace won't be under that sort of pressure and, consequently, will only review and update its action plans annually.

There are however, some circumstances where the generation of a strategic plan is a must, whatever the pressures and constraints might be. For you must do a strategic plan when your organisation is:

- just getting started, or
- preparing for a new major venture.

In both of these situations, your strategic plan will be a part of a larger package; one that might also contain, for example, a marketing plan, financial plan and an operational plan. You'll also need to consider size or novelty issues here. For example, developing a new department, a large retail outlet, or a major new product will require a strategic plan whereas creating a 'clone' of an existing product or retail outlet may not.

Your strategic plan – how?

Earlier in this chapter you saw that all plans contain:

- a specific outcome or objective, and
- a set of linked intended actions aimed at achieving that outcome.

You also saw in Figure 4.1 that the shift from vision to targets means:

- more detail, and
- shorter timescales.

In the rest of this chapter, you'll be reading about the ways and means of your strategic plan's creation. But that isn't all that you'll need to do and in the following chapter (Chapter 5 – What do we do next?) you'll be reading about how to carry out, monitor, control and complete that plan.

But now you'll need to take a look at the steps and stages that you'll go through to get to success in the process of creating your strategic plan – a plan that aims to shift your vision from 'hoped for' to 'achieved'.

Steps and stages

Let's be clear about one thing, right at the start of this section – that there isn't a unique and special process for creating your strategic plan. 'It all depends', as they say. In your case, it'll depend on things like how many people you employ or are in your workgroup and what sort of relationships you have with these co-workers and your clients or customers. It'll also be influenced by the way that your organisation or workgroup handles planning and the patterns of communication that you have. Nevertheless, you'll have to make a 'clear-cut' decision about which way is right for you and that will involve you in deciding:

- how you intend to proceed, and
- who's involved.

So, let's look at these interlinked factors in more detail.

Process, what process?

You've quite a range of options here. You can, for example, decide to have a series of once-a-week half-day meetings with a team of people and then, finally, delegate the drafting of the document that defines your strategic plan to a member of this team. If you're going down this route do remember that attendance at these meetings will be a 'must-do' – no excuses accepted – situation and that, as a result, most of your team will now have to do in four-and-a-half-days what they used to do in five days. The stresses, strains and feelings that will result from this may take you down the route of deciding to start with a 'Strategy Weekend' – a day or two away from the work environment that might start with strategy brainstorming sessions and finish with an agreed and consensus generated agreement for what happens next. Whether this consensus will 'stick' depends upon another factor that you'll need to consider carefully – who was involved in its generation (see below). Overall, you should aim to complete your planning process within two months with meetings being held no more than two to three weeks apart. Take any longer than that and you'll lose momentum and participant interest.

Don't forget that this planning comes at a cost – of staff time and resources – together with the cost of what's given up or not done so that your plan is created. A key point here is that if your organisation has cash flow or other problems these need to be sorted out *before* you start your strategic planning process. Try to do them both and you'll succeed with neither.

Who's involved?

There are three issues here.

The first of these is that you don't have to do it on your own. Doing that is potentially dangerous – both to you (because of the workload involved) and to your organisation or workgroup (because you don't know it all). There are circumstances – such as when you haven't done this sort of planning before or when previous strategic planning has failed or when no one has the necessary facilitation skills – where using a consultant can help. However, do choose your consultant with care, making sure that he or she has the necessary skills and experience and is able to act impartially.

The second issue is about making sure that the people involved in your core strategic planning team have the analytical and intellectual skills that will be needed. A mix of blue-sky thinkers, creative problem solvers and people with a solid practical experience of the 'nitty-gritty' is good – if you can get it.

The third issue is about the how and when of stakeholder involvement. You met this issue in Chapter 2 – What's it all about? but it's worth reminding you that a stakeholder is, according to those who know about these things, *'a person, group, organisation, or system who affects or can be affected by an organisation's actions'.* That throws a pretty wide net, doesn't it?

Nevertheless, these stakeholders are important. Get them 'on-board' in your journey towards your vision and you'll find that they'll provide help and support. Doing this means that your strategic planning needs to involve or take account of – in one way or another – the opinions of a wide range of people. These can be key employees, your accountant, heads of other departments, your bank manager, board members – and, of course, external stakeholders such customers, clients, advisers and consultants. How and when you do this will, of course depend on their 'zone of influence'. For example, your bank manager and your accountant will need to be involved when you're into the capital and cash flow implications of your plan. If there's likely to be a limit on capital availability you'll need to know this early – rather than late.

The plan

Once it's written, your strategic plan should identify a clear and well-defined route that you're going to follow in order to reach your vision. To get to that point – a completed plan – you'll have asked and answered three key questions:

Where are you now?

In Chapter 3 – Who's got the map? – you saw that the day-by-day operations of your organisation or workplace are about converting resources into products or services. You also saw that the efficiency, effectiveness and adaptability of these operations should be DUMB – as in Doable, Understandable, Manageable and Beneficial – and SMART – as in Specific, Measurable, Attainable, Realistic and Time-based.

You also saw that you assess the internal and external environments that your organisation or workplace operates in by doing PESTLE and SWOT analyses. If you want to add more flesh to these analyses you can consider doing what Michael Porter calls a 'Five Forces' audit (see Further Information and Reading).

Bring all of these together and you should have a clear picture of how your business, organisation or work unit:

- operates internally
- achieves its profitability, and
- compares with competitors.

You should generate this in a written form, making sure that, when you do, it's realistic, detached and critical. You should also review it periodically.

Where do you want to go to?

You've already got the answer to this question – it's your vision (see Chapters 2 and 3). There you read about the process of working out what your vision is about and deciding where you want your organisation or workplace to be in the future. This vision is the foundation stone of your strategic plan and without it you, as they say, 'ain't going no place'.

However, this word 'vision' can, and does, often get confused with another similar word – ' mission'. So let's spend a little time to make sure that you understand the differences between them. Vision, as you know, is defined as *'a concise summary of where you see your business, organisation or workplace in five to ten years' time'* whereas a mission statement is *'a written declaration of a firm's core purpose and focus.'* What this tells you is that, at their respective cores, a vision is about the *future* and a mission is about the *present*. If you haven't got a mission statement, generating one is worth the time and effort – providing it's done by consensus and, also, providing you don't confuse it with your vision. Take a look at Table 4.1 to see examples of some current mission statements.

Table 4.1: Mission statements

Starbucks: 'Our mission is to inspire and nurture the human spirit – one person, one cup, one neighbourhood at a time.'

BBC: 'To enrich people's lives with programmes and services that inform, educate and entertain.'

Virgin Atlantic: 'To grow a profitable airline where people love to fly and where people love to work.'

How will you get there?

There's only one answer to this question – and that, believe or not, is that you'll get to where you want to go by developing a plan. But this plan, if it's going to succeed, must be:

- simple but concrete
- detailed enough to make it meaningful and usable but not so detailed that it becomes unnecessarily complicated

- easily understood by all who use it
- easy to change, update and revise
- easily used to monitor project progress, and
- easy to use as a means of communication.

But that's not all that you need from your strategic plan.

A good plan will not only have all these characteristics, it will also be able to do something else. For it will draw in and act as a focusing 'lens' for the skills, abilities and energy of the people who become engaged in completing it. Create a plan that can do all of this and you're more than halfway towards success. Fail – and give yourself a plan that's difficult to understand or full of irrelevant detail or slow and difficult to update – then you'll not only have a problem; you'll also have a dying vision!

So let's get started on your plan.

Your strategic plan

The management guru Henry Mintzberg once said that the act of planning is, at its core, about decision taking. The sort of decisions that you'll have to take in order to create the plan that'll convert your vision from hope to reality are the ones that'll spring from the answers to the following questions:

- What actions are needed to reach that vision within the given timespan?
- How much money is needed?
- When do these actions need to start and finish?
- Who will carry out these actions?
- What equipment, tools and materials are needed?

The answers to these questions contain the details of the future actions of your plan – a plan that's particular to you and your vision.

One way of handling this situation is to treat the task of achieving your vision as a project. When you think about this you'll soon realise that doing that makes a lot of sense. For a project:

- is about change
- is, in some way, unique
- has a limited and defined period time-span
- has defined outcomes or targets
- uses a variety of resources
- involves risk and, last but not least,
- needs people.

To convert the broad-brush strokes of your vision into a project you're going to have to start by identifying the actions needed. In the lexicon of project management this is called creating a Work Breakdown Schedule (WBS). The level of detail that's contained in the WBS of your strategic action plan is important. Too much and you'll finish with a plan that's unmanageable – because it's far too detailed. Too little and you'll finish up with a plan that is so broad-brush that it serves little purpose. In general, it's best to limit the activities shown in your plan to those that have durations greater than about 5 per cent of the plan's total duration. What this means is that on a five-year or 260-week duration plan you'll not show activities with durations of 13 weeks or less. However, don't forget that there will be some significant but short duration activities that you'll have to include such as those that:

- signal a transfer of responsibility – such as handovers or completions, or
- are so important that they have to be included – such as getting planning permission or authorisation to proceed.

Once you've generated your Strategic WBS you will begin to see the way that these individual actions influence each other. Some of these actions, for example, can't be started until other actions are finished. In the jargon of project planning this is called 'interdependency'.

Estimating how long it will take to do something or duration of an activity has been described as a mixture of science, experience and intuition. But, when a project takes you beyond the boundaries of your prior experience or easily accessible information, then it's time to get more professional help.

Once you've got your activity duration estimate information together then you'll be ready to take the next step – that of generating the first draft of the plan that will link all of these together: your strategic action plan. But before you do that you need to remember that not only does this plan act as a record of your intentions; it also acts as a way of presenting these intentions and your decisions about them to all of the people that are involved in or have an interest in your project.

Most information is best presented in a visual form and the project plan is no exception. One of the oldest and simplest forms of the project plan is the bar chart or Gantt chart. This has:

- a horizontal time scale
- a vertical list of activities
- a horizontal line or bar for each activity.

The lengths of these horizontal bars are proportional to the time needed to complete the activity (see Figure 4.3).

A chart like this, with its time scale base and visual representation of activity duration and completion, will give you a clear and easily understandable picture of the project. It's also one that you can use to communicate with others and to see the sequence of activities that make up the project 'critical path'. This is the chain of linked events that leads to the shortest project completion time. It's also a sequence of events in which delay will lead to the delay of the whole project rather than just a delay of a single activity. Seeing this helps you to manage the project. You can, for example, decide to divert resources into a critical path activity and, by so doing, further reduce the project completion time. It also tells you which of the project's activities you need to focus your attention on if you are to complete the project on time.

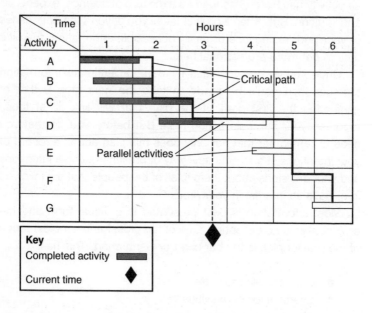

Figure 4.3: Gantt chart

All of this not only helps you to manage your project, it also helps you to do that efficiently and effectively. Whichever way you use to display your strategic action plan it's vital that you make sure that it effectively addresses and specifies the goals, objectives and activities involved.

But an action plan like this isn't the only sort of plan that you'll need to develop. For you'll also need the following.

Expenditure plan or budget

Money is the life blood of all projects – whatever their outcome might be. You're going to need to create a budget for your strategic plan. This – once you've created it – should tell you not only the total spend involved in reaching your vision, it should also tell you:

- what the money is spent on (salaries, rent, utilities, equipment etc.)
- when it's spent.

Doing this isn't as difficult as it sounds – take a look at *Instant Manager: Project Management* if you want more detail about how to do this (see Further Information and Reading).

HR or human resource plan

In this plan you'll need to identify, by name, the important individuals and groups with a description of their roles and responsibilities on the project. You'll also need to know about total people numbers and skills needed to complete the project. A good HR plan will identify start dates, estimated durations and sources.

Communications plan

This should tell anybody who reads it about who needs to be kept informed about the project and how they will receive that information. Weekly or monthly progress reports are a good idea providing they describe how the project is performing, milestones achieved and work planned for the next period.

Risk management plan

Risk management is an important and often neglected part of strategic planning. For that reason there's a whole chapter devoted to it later in the book (see Chapter 6 – Do you take the risk?).

Monitoring plan

Once your strategic action plan gets underway you'll need to monitor its progress. There's quite a lot about this in the next chapter (see Chapter 5 – What do we do next?)

Looks like a lot work, doesn't it? In reality, however, most of these plans can each be described on a single sheet of paper; sheets that you'll then integrate into a final all-encompassing document that summarises the results and decisions of the strategic planning process. There's no set format for this document but do be sure that it includes:

- an executive summary preferably located at the beginning, and
- the outcomes of each major step.

Chapter checklist

In this chapter you've taken a look at the process of identifying the actions and the resources needed to enable and support your vision's journey from where you are now to where you want to be. Use the list below to check where you've got to. If you've missed something or don't understand it go back to the page given and read through it again.

- Twenty-first-century business world plans can be about almost anything (page 59).
- Most of these are formal written down plans (page 60).
- Business strategy is about:
  - direction – where *is* the business going ?
  - time scale – undoubtedly long-term but with medium- and short-term implications
  - markets – which ones and why?
  - advantage – what's your advantage?
  - resources – what do you need to make sure that you'll win?
  - externals – what environmental and stakeholder pressures and influences are about? (page 62).
- The benefits of having a strategic plan include:
  - specific goals and objectives
  - focus on the important things
  - a road map for your vision's route from idea to reality
  - plan sharing with work colleagues
  - finding out about your organisation's: strengths and weaknesses; opportunities and threats.
  - knowing about: the areas in which you need help; when to go with your strengths; the threats you need to guard against; the opportunities you need to grasp (page 63).
- When you do your strategic planning depends upon:
  - what sort of an organisation you're in
  - what's happening in that organisation (page 64).
- You'll need to make your own choice about the process that you use and the people that you involve (pages 68–69).
- Your strategic plan must be:
  - a bridge between intention and reality for your vision
  - simple but concrete
  - detailed enough to make it meaningful and usable but not so much detail that it becomes unnecessarily complicated

- easily understood by all who use it
- easy to change, update and revise
- easily used to monitor project progress, and
- easy to use as a means of communication (page 72).
● The document that records your strategic plan will contain other plans including:
  - strategic action plan
  - expenditure plan or budget
  - HR or human resource plan
  - communications plan
  - risk management plan, and
  - monitoring plan (pages 73–78).

Skills checkout

Doing, rather than just reading about, the things that you've been reading about in this chapter will be yet another demanding but worthwhile task. You will need to continue to develop, refine and expand your individual 'bundle' of skills. If you think about what you've read you soon realise that these will include skills such as:

analysing	risk assessment
planning	risk management
involving others	networking
decision making	influencing and persuading
delegating	communicating
innovating	consulting
setting objectives	prioritising
thinking strategically	balancing competing needs
	negotiating

All of these are needed for Unit B3 of the Providing Direction section of the UK National Occupational Standards for Management and Leadership.

05

What do we do next?

This chapter will tell you about the why, how and when of implementing your strategic plan. It will do that by looking at the ways that you'll use to monitor and control your plan, take the decisions needed and solve the problems that will come up on its road to completion.

Ready, steady, GO!

You're on your way!

You've taken your first step towards achieving your vision and, with that, all sorts of things start to happen. Most, but not all, of these will be actions that you'd chosen and planned. But you'll also find that some of the risks that you'd previously dismissed as unlikely or remote also spring into life. These will show themselves in all sorts of ways – promises that aren't kept, deliveries that are delayed or the breakdown of a vital piece of equipment. When things like this happen, your ability to start and complete the actions that you'd chosen and planned will be challenged. As a result, the outcome of your strategic plan – your vision – will be put at risk.

In the next chapter (Chapter 6 – Do you take the risk?) you'll read about how you can use risk management to limit both the occurrence and the effects of these unwanted events. But what you need, here and now, is a special package of skills and abilities; one that you can use to keep your progress through your strategic plan 'on-track'. It's a package that, used well, will:

- tell you when the activities of your project are drifting 'off-track'
- help you to identify the reasons for this, and
- help you find out what you can do about this.

In short, it's a package that you'll use to monitor and control your project.

Monitoring

Take a look in the *Oxford English Dictionary* and you'll find that when you monitor something you *'observe or supervise it, or keep it under review – often by measuring or testing it at regular intervals.'*

The objective of doing this is an obvious one. For monitoring, if it's done effectively and accurately, will tell you whether your actual actions are – or aren't – achieving the aims and objectives that you laid out in your strategic plan. But that's not the only reason for your monitoring. For it – or rather the information it provides – will:

- enable you to predict where you and your plan are likely to be in the future
- provide you with the means to inform and motivate your strategic plan's 'stakeholders'.

But that's not all that it will give you. For, used well, your monitoring will also tell you about the causes of your project's drifts and deviations. This information will enable you to begin to do something about the cause of these differences – to solve your strategic plan's problems – and thus bring it back 'on track'.

Monitoring – what and when?

When it comes to monitoring there are two key decisions that you have to make right at the beginning. These are:

- what you're going to monitor, and
- when or how often you're going to monitor it.

So, let's look at each of these in turn.

What

The key to success in the 'what' of your monitoring lies in the numbers of things that you monitor. Too many and you'll finish up with too much data and too little time to analyse it. Too few and you'll miss the drift or movement away from your plan – and not be able to react to correct it until it is too late. Getting the balance right is important, and if you're going to do that you're going to have to identify your plan's 'pulse points'. These 'pulse points' must be related to the key features of your plan – its cost, its outcome and its duration. The closer that the relationship is, the better your monitoring will be. But if those 'pulse points' are going to help you to achieve your vision they must also be:

- significant
- believable, and
- easy to measure and understand.

Finding 'pulse points' like this isn't always easy but it can be done. For example, on a project to write a book like this the number of words written and the timescale of that writing would be key pulse points. You need to be able to link and compare the information that your pulse-point measurement gives you to both your action plan and your cost budget. Doing this will help you to decide the other key aspect of your monitoring – when or how often you do it. You'll also, as you'll see in the next chapter of this book, need to monitor the risks associated with your strategic project.

When

Deciding when you do your monitoring is just as important as deciding what to monitor. Too often and you'll drown in data; not often enough and you'll miss the early drift that leads to major problems later. Getting it right depends on things like the overall duration of your plan and the risks involved in it. On long duration plans, for example, measurement and reporting on a weekly frequency would usually be OK. On a short duration plan – in which the events of a single day can be crucial – measurement and reporting on a daily or even half-daily frequency will be needed. Similarly, high-risk projects demand, for obvious reasons, more frequent measurements than low risk projects. Whatever you decide, do remember that being regular in your monitoring will keep you in touch with your strategic plan – and that is what you'll need if you're going to achieve your vision.

Monitoring and your strategic plan

In the previous chapter (Chapter 4 – Can you see where we're going?) you read that your project's plan is your attempt to control the future of your vision. Now, with your project underway, this plan becomes a road map for your project's journey, a 'this-is-what-you-do-next' guide for the actions of all involved.

But that isn't all that your strategic plan can do for you. You can also use that plan as a baseline against which you can monitor the progress of your vision on its road to completion. To do this you'll need to get down to the 'nitty-gritty' of what's happening. You'll need to compare the actual achieved timing and duration of activities to those of your original plan or schedule. Sometimes this will show you that activities are ahead of schedule and other times that they are behind. When either of these happens you'll need to decide what you are going to do. Your plan will help you to do that. For it will provide a framework within which you can identify and evaluate the options or choices that are available to you. To achieve this your plan must – as you saw in Chapter 4 – be clear, unambiguous, easily understood and, above all, capable of change. This act of changing or modifying your project plan is one of the ways by which you can control your project. But if that change is to be effective then it must always be preceded by and based on the data generated by the process of monitoring.

This data can be presented and contained within the project plan itself, as you saw in Figure 4.3 with the filled-in bars of a Gantt chart. Using the milestones of your plan is another way of presenting monitoring information. These milestones are best set at the end or beginning of an activity – for ease of identification – and are usually limited to Critical Path activities. As you saw in Figure 4.3 they are shown on a Gantt chart by an icon (◇) with the unfilled ◆ representing a scheduled milestone and the filled, a completed milestone. You can also use a milestone report:

Milestone No.	Scheduled Date	Anticipated Date	Achieved Date	Notes
4	25 April	–	23 April	Completed ahead of schedule
5	13 Jan.	15 Jan	–	Material delivery delay anticipated

These project milestones will tell you, as do the milestones of our highways and roads, how far you have travelled towards the completion of your project. But they aren't the only tools that you can use to monitor the status of your project and you'll get more information about other tools that you can use when you read some of the books listed at the end of this book (see Further Information and Reading).

Monitoring and your budget

In Chapter 4 you saw that you'll need to develop an expenditure plan or budget; a plan or budget that will tell you about the total spend needed to reach your vision and the 'on what' (salaries, rent, utilities, equipment, etc.) and the 'when' of your spend.

Monitoring the cash flow of your strategic plan is an absolute must. The S curve (Figure 5.1) is one of the ways by which you can do this. This gets its name – S curve – from the fact that the plot of the budgeted cumulative cost usually follows an S shape. When you look at Figure 5.1 you'll see that, when used to monitor your costs, it shows the plots of the project's cumulative budget and actual spends against time. This enables you to see the differences between these spends and that tells you whether you are spending more or less than was budgeted.

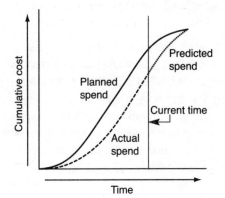

Figure 5.1: The S curve

In the example shown in Figure 5.1 you'll see that, currently, the cumulative actual cost of your project is less than you had planned – an apparently comfortable situation, you might think.

But this may not be so! This situation could have come about because:

- the work completed was on schedule or even ahead of schedule but was costing less than you had planned, or
- the work completed was behind schedule but was costing more than had been planned.

The differences between these two are significant. For one of them – the lower than budgeted achieved cost – means that your future costs are likely to be less than the budgeted level while the other – the higher than budgeted achieved cost – means that your future costs look likely to exceed the budget.

But which one is it?

Earned value

Earned Value Analysis (EVA) is probably the best way of answering this question – and telling you what is actually happening. EVA is a widely accepted practice that's used to measure the progress of projects against the baseline of their project budget and plan. It may, at first glance, seem complicated. But it's not and using it can add a powerful boost to your strategic project management skills. EVA uses three basic measures that are based on the actual costs incurred and cost estimates for your project (see Table 5.1).

Table 5.1: EVA measures

Projected or Planned Value (PV)
This cost answers the question: 'How much did you expect to pay for the work scheduled to be done by now?' It's also called the **Budgeted Cost of Work Scheduled** (BCWS).

Earned Value (EV)
This cost answers the question: 'How much did you expect to pay for the work that was actually done by now?' It's also called the **Budgeted Cost of Work Performed** (BCWP).

Actual Cost (AC)
This cost answers the question: 'What was the actual cost of the work completed by now? It's also called the **Actual Cost of Work Performed** (ACWP).

These costs are used to calculate a set of variances:

- **Schedule Variance (SV)**

    This will give you the answer to the question: 'Are you ahead of or behind schedule?' and is calculated as follows:

    SV = EV – PV or

    SV = BCWP – BCWS

    A negative value for SV means that you are behind schedule.

- **Cost Variance (CV)**

    This will give you the answer to the question: 'Are you spending more or less than budget?' and is calculated as follows:

    CV = EV – AC or

    CV = BCWP – ACWP

    A negative value means that you are over budget.

You can see all of these in Figure 5.2 below.

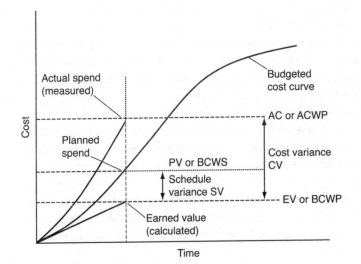

Figure 5.2: EVA chart

You can also use your Projected or Planned Value (PV), Earned Value (EV) and Actual Cost (AC) to give you an indication of how you stand with respect to both your schedule and your budget. You'll do this by calculating two ratios – Schedule Performance Index (SPI) and Cost Performance Index (CPI). To see how you can calculate and use these indices to give you even more information about your progress towards the completion of your strategic plan you'll need to take a look at *Instant Manager: Project Management* and the other project management books listed in Further Information and Reading at the end of the book.

Do you have a problem?

Problems are astonishingly common events. They appear everywhere – at work, home and at play. So, you shouldn't be surprised when you meet problems in your strategic plan project. These can be about almost anything and they can be huge, tiny, significant, trivial, complex or simple. They'll all have the potential to limit your ability to achieve a desired goal or objective. You will, of course, have subjected the more predictable of these problems to the rigours of your risk management procedures and hence avoided them or reduced their impact (see Chapter 6 – Do you take the risk?). But there will always be problems that are unpredictable.

So what can you do when these appear?

The answer here is that you need to stand back and take a good hard look at the information that you have about your problem. Ask yourself questions like 'Have I seen this problem before?' and 'What appear to be the problem's potential consequences?' You'll need to be methodical about doing this. Write down all that you know about the situation. Your aim, when you do this, will be to get answers to the following questions:

- What is happening?
- Where is it happening?
- When is it happening? and, if you can:
- Why is it happening?

When you've done that you'll probably find that the problem has changed its appearance. What had appeared to be a supplier or a planning problem might now, for example, turn out to be a labour or productivity problem. Getting focused like this does help. It means that the time that you have can now be applied in a much more focused way and by using the ways and means of project problem solving.

Project problem solving – ways

At its core, the act of solving a problem is about bridging a gap – the gap between where your strategic plan project is and where it ought to be. You'll have found out about this gap by comparing the results of your monitoring and the intentions of your project plan and budget. But having these two essential 'bits' of information won't tell you how to solve your problem. Nor will it tell you how to best use the limited time and resources that you have available. The first step towards solving your problem is that you get realistic about what can be achieved with the limited time and information that you have. Getting to an optimum solution can take a lot of time and money whereas settling for a 'good-enough' or adequate solution – even for a major problem – does mean that you can get the project back 'on-track'.

Doing this is called 'satisficing'. This involves using a decision-making strategy that attempts to generate an adequate solution, rather than identify an optimal one. The verb 'to satisfice' was coined by Herbert Simon, an American social scientist, and to do it you'll first need to decide what's the minimum that you'll accept as a solution to your problem. An example of this would be deciding to get your stalled car running again on a cold and windy winter's night rather than running a full diagnostic as to why it stalled in the first place. Once you've made this decision you'll need to start looking, one at a time, at the alternative solutions to your problem. The first of these that matches your minimum solution – getting the car running again – is the one that you'll accept and implement. Research tells us that doing this is a very common way of solving problems in organisations.

But whether you satisfice or rigorously evaluate all of the options available to you to solve your problem the basic process that you'll follow will be the same. This is illustrated in Figure 5.3.

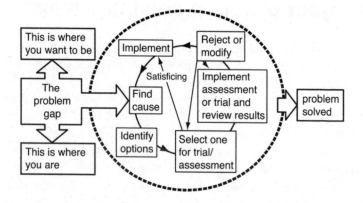

Figure 5.3: The problem-solving cycle

When you look at Figure 5.3, you'll see that, in its fullest form, your problem-solving process has six steps and stages:

1. What caused the problem gap? Find an answer.
2. How can you close the gap? Identify your potential solutions.
3. Which one shall we use? Select one for trial.
4. Does it work? Do the trial and review its results.
5. Will it do? Modify, accept or reject that solution as required.
6. Implement the solution.

Getting all of this right is important; it can make the difference between success and failure in your problem solving. So let's look at each of these in turn.

Step 1: What caused the gap?

Your project monitoring has told you that there's a gap – you've overspent or it's taking longer than you'd planned. You need to find out what's causing this gap. You can do this in a number of ways – by using rigorous number-based analysis or statistics or by using less rigorous, but just as effective, 'creative' methods. You can do it in a team or on your own and you can use a wide range of techniques – such as Pareto analysis, Ishikawa diagrams and Diagramming – to help you. Some of these listed in Table 5.2 and you'll find detailed descriptions of how to use these and other techniques in *Instant Manager: Project Management* (see Further Information and Reading). The danger here is that you'll think that you need to find out about everything that's involved. That isn't necessary – as someone, somewhere, once said, 'Don't wait until you have all the answers.' Keep in mind that in this step it's causes, rather than solutions, that you are looking for. If you overanalyse – by trying to get *all* the answers – you'll delay solving your problem.

Table 5.2: Problem-solving techniques

Ishikawa, Fishbone or Cause and Effect technique

Input/output diagramming

Brainstorming

Nominal group technique

Lateral thinking

Moving average

CUSUM or Cumulative Sum

What, Where, When, Who and How

Force field analysis

Pareto analysis

Multiple cause diagram

Step 2: Can you close the gap?

This step is about identifying what your options are for closing the gap. There are several methods that you can use to do this. You'll probably have met and used some of these before – such as brainstorming and nominal group technique. Other techniques – such as force field analysis – may be new to you. Again, you'll find detailed descriptions of these and other techniques in *Instant Manager: Project Management* (see Further Information and Reading). It's your choice – but whichever technique or tool you use, you'll still need the same outcome – a number of options for what you do next. What you have to do then is decide which of these you are going to try out.

Step 3: Which one shall I use?

Step 2 has given you a choice – which of the list of potential solutions do you try out? The words of the Japanese quality guru, Shigeo Shingo, are going to help here. For he tells us to 'think smart and think small'. You'll use this wisdom by choosing the solution that's:

- the simplest, or
- the most efficient, or
- the most economical.

But if you're going to take the 'satisficing' route and choose the first potential solution that satisfies you then you'll jump from this step to Step 6.

Whichever way you do it, remember that there's an element of risk whichever option you choose – and use your risk management procedure (see Chapter 6 – Do you take the risk?) to check it out.

Step 4: Does it work?

In this step you'll aim to find out whether your chosen option will close the gap between where your project currently is and where you want it to be. Again, you can do this in a number of ways: by undertaking a small-scale trial of that option, by using numbers or by using the 'what if' facility of your plan to work out the cost and consequences of the option. You'll almost certainly be short on time and money so if you go the trial route you'll need to carefully plan and monitor that trial. The results of that trial should give you answers to questions like these:

- Was the option close to achieving the desired result?
- If not, why not?
- Are you satisfied that you've identified all the costs and consequences of the chosen option?

Step 5: Will it do?

When you review the results of this trial you'll be able to see whether the option that you chose back in Step 3 has generated a solution to your problem. But there will be times when these results don't meet your expectations. Then you'll have to decide whether to drop that option and go back to Step 3 to choose another or to modify the first option and then go back to Step 4 to re-assess or re-trial it.

Step 6: Implementation

You will have got to this step because:

- during Step 5 you decided to implement the solution you had chosen and then trialed in Steps 3 and 4, or
- in Step 3 you decided to take the 'satisficing' route, chose the first potential solution that satisfied you and then jumped to this step.

Whichever route you took to get here it's worth reminding yourself that this implementation will need to be planned and monitored with care and forethought.

Decisions, Decisions, Decisions

You've probably noticed by now that there's a lot of decision taking going on during the implementation of your vision's strategic plan. Taking a decision is a key skill whatever your role might be and for that reason it's worth taking a brief look at the 'why' and 'how' of decision making.

Decision making – why?

Decision making is a cognitive process. That is it's based on and uses your thought patterns. You'll use it when you're faced with:

- uncertainty, and
- several alternative courses of action.

Its outcome is, not surprisingly, a decision. This usually takes the form of an action or an opinion. If you think about this you'll soon see that the decision-making process gets used a lot. Your decisions can be about almost anything – what to eat or drink, whether to cross the road, what clothes to wear, whether to invest in a new venture, etc. Because of this there's been a lot of research conducted into the 'how' and 'why' of decision taking. This tells us that the decision-making process kicks into action when you come face to face with uncertainty. This uncertainty can be real, imagined or anticipated. Your decision will aim to reduce this uncertainty and your concerns will be about whether the decision that you make will lead to benefit or harm. As such your decisions will be influenced by your emotions as well as your logic.

Decision making – how?

Decision making is a complex process that research tells us draws on information, emotions and beliefs. Here's an outline of the steps and stages that you go through during the process of making a decision:

1. **You decide what the decision's about** – this is about issues such as scope and limitations.
2. **You get as many facts as you can** – including your feelings, hunches and intuitions and the views of those who will be affected by your decision or will have to implement it.
3. **You develop alternatives** – a list of all the possible choices you have, including doing nothing.
4. **You evaluate each alternative** – negatives (cost, consequences, problems created, time needed, etc.) and positives (money saved, time saved, added creativity, better morale, etc.).
5. **You rate the risks involved in each alternative** – see Chapter 6 – Do you take the risk?
6. **Decision time!** – you choose what to do.

Remember that the outcome of this process – your decision – will only be as good as:

- the quality and extent of the information it's based upon
- how well (or badly) you implement that decision
- whether people agree with the decision and understand what it means.

It's also worth remembering that, if time or other resources are in short supply, you can satisfice. As you saw earlier in this chapter this involves accepting the first alternative that you come across that meets a set of minimum criteria.

Chapter checklist

Use the list below to check out where you've got to. If you've missed something or didn't understand it go back to the page given and read it through again.

- Monitoring will tell you whether your plan is or isn't 'on track' (page 82).
- Your monitor must be:
  - significant
  - believable
  - easy to measure and understand (page 83).
- How often you monitor must reflect the duration and risk level of your project (page 84).
- Regular monitoring will keep you in touch with your project (page 84).
- Monitoring can use milestone reports and the bars of your Gantt chart (page 85).
- Monitoring your project's cash flow is important and can use S curves or Earned Value Analysis (pages 86–90).
- Write down the what, where, when and why of your problem (page 91).
- Remember that you don't have to find the optimal solution and that satisficing will find you an 'adequate' solution (page 91).
- Make sure that you understand and can use the problem-solving cycle (page 92).
- Find out about and learn to use problem-solving techniques such as Ishikawa, Fishbone or cause and effect, brainstorming, lateral thinking and Pareto analysis and other techniques (page 93).
- You'll make decisions when you're faced with:
  - uncertainty, and
  - several alternative courses of action (page 97).

- The steps and stages of decision making are:
    1. Decide what the decision's about.
    2. Get as many facts as you can.
    3. Develop alternatives.
    4. Evaluate each alternative.
    5. Rate each alternative's risks.
    6. Decision time! (page 98).
- Your decision will only be as good as:
    - the quality and extent of the information it's based upon
    - how well (or badly) you implement that decision
    - whether people agree with the decision and understand what it means (page 98).

Skills checkout

If you're going to do the things that you've been reading about in this chapter you'll need to continue to develop, refine and expand your individual 'bundle' of skills. If you think about what you've read you'll soon realise that these will include skills such as:

risk assessment/management	planning
influencing and persuading	delegating
communicating	involving others
networking	decision making
monitoring	consulting
innovating	thinking strategically
balancing competing needs	evaluating
managing and presenting information	problem solving

All of these are needed for Unit B4 of the Providing Direction section of the UK National Occupational Standards for Management and Leadership.

06

Do you take the risk?

This chapter starts by looking at the nature and origins of risk and then moves on to see how risk figures in, and is important to, the process of leading people. Finally, you'll take a look at the process of risk management – with its steps of identifying, analysing, evaluating and treating risk.

So let's start by taking a look, firstly, at the what, when and where of risk and then, secondly, at exactly what's meant by risk.

Risks – what, when and where?

Uncertainty and its close cousin risk are ever-present factors in all of our lives – they just never seem to go away. They are there whatever we do, wherever or whenever we do it. Try as we may to reduce the uncertainty in our lives, there will always be events and choices that we hadn't foreseen and information we'd missed or that wasn't available when we needed it. All of these come together to create risk.

Human beings have been taking risks for a long, long time and will continue to do so into the far and distant future. You do it when you drive through a traffic light on amber, smoke a cigarette, eat butter instead of low-fat spread or bet money on the result of a horse race or football game. In your workplace you take a risk when you decide to invest in new technology, drill for oil, launch a new product, publish a new book or open a different sort of supermarket. These risks pop up, like many-headed hydra, in every part of your life. As such, they get described in an incredibly diverse range of ways, with adjectives such as personal, corporate, technical, medical, financial, business, marketing, environmental and political in regular use.

Nevertheless, despite all of this diversity, the process of taking a risk is, at its core, the same wherever and whenever you do it. For risk is always:

- associated with uncertainty
- coupled with a potential or proposed future action
- shifted from the abstract to the real when a decision is taken.

This decision – about what you'll do in the future – is always taken after you've balanced – consciously or unconsciously – what you see as the potential rewards of your decision against what you see as its potential unfavourable results. Once the decision is taken, you can move forward, take the action and meet the uncertainties of the future. Until you do that – take the risk – there can be no reward or progress. But, as you'll see later in this chapter, it's important to make sure that these risks are managed effectively. So, let's start your journey towards understanding how you can manage risk – by deciding exactly what risk is.

Risk – what does it mean?

The doyen of dictionaries – the *Oxford English Dictionary* – tells us that in the Middle Ages the word risk had its roots in the French word *'risque'* and had a negative meaning of *'a hazard, danger; exposure to mischance or peril'*. However, when you probe further back into history you'll find broader meanings for risk. These relate 'risk' to actions such as 'seeking prosperity' and outcomes such as 'good and bad fortune'. You'll also see that risk is a word that had, in the past, been used in specific ways – as, for example, in relation to shipping and the consequences of loss and damage at sea. Move towards more contemporary times and you'll find that, by the eighteenth century, risk had become associated with the mathematics of probability. As a result definitions (for risk) began to say that it was about the expected value of one or more results of one or more future events. One result of this change was the definition below:

Risk = (probability of an event occurring) × (the impact of that event)

This sort of definition is still used in techniques such as Probabilistic Risk Assessment (PRA) which are used by the nuclear, aerospace and chemical industries. By the 1990s this sort of technique was being used by bankers in the form of a 'value-at-risk' or VAR technique aimed at assessing how much money the bank could expect to lose under adverse market conditions. At the same time far looser and exclusively negative definitions for risk began to appear, such as:

'the probability and magnitude of a loss, disaster or other undesirable event'
or
'something bad could happen'

and behavioural concepts such as risk averse, risk neutral and risk-seeking (or risk-loving) (see Table 6.1) made their appearance.

Table 6.1: Attitudes to risk

Risk averse: avoids risk unless adequately compensated for it.

Risk neutral: insensitive or indifferent to risk.

Risk loving: has a preference for risk.

However, all of this changed in November 2009 with the release of the first international risk management standard – *ISO 31000:2009 Risk Management – Principles and Guidelines (ISO 31000)*. Based upon and replacing an earlier Australian and New Zealand standard (*AS/NZS 4360:2004 Risk Management*) and drawing on the skills and knowledge of risk experts from 28 countries, this standard 'moved the goalposts' when it came to risk definition. For risk, it tells us, is *'the effect of uncertainty on objectives'*.

As we're going to use this definition throughout the rest of this chapter it's worth spending a little time looking at it. When you do that you'll soon notice that it's a definition about 'effect' rather than the 'chance' or 'probability'. Probe a bit further and you'll find that it's a definition that's neutral – it allows for the existence of both negative and positive consequences. Later in this chapter you'll go on to look in more detail at the risk management process described in this standard. But before you do that you need to take a look at the relationship between leadership and risk.

Risk and leadership

You've already seen, in earlier chapters of this book, that the process of leading or directing people in an organisation is one that, like risk taking, is about future actions. It aims, as you saw, to:

- influence, inspire and motivate people

- do so by establishing a direction, target or vision for
  these people's future collective efforts.

Doing this – being a leader – is an inherently risky business. For leading is about initiating, blazing new trails, venturing into unmapped territory – all of which are actions that contain high levels of implicit risk. But you've already seen in Chapter 2 – What's it all about? – that this act of leading is no longer the exclusive prerogative of those who sit at the tops of our organisations. It's an act that has permeated down through the hierarchical layers of our organisations. As a consequence, leading (together with its attendant risks) is no longer exclusively associated with initiating new ventures or creating new visions. It's also become associated with the day-to-day tasks of directing and working with others. This, together with the shift towards the leaner, flatter organisations of the twenty-first century (see Chapter 11 – What comes next?), has created a work-a-day world in which there just isn't time to consult upwards and where achieving high levels of customer service often means taking a risk.

However, this doesn't always happen because:

- people aren't sure that their bosses will support them if the risk goes bad and things don't turn out right
- very few organisations celebrate risk taking
- middle managers don't like the idea of 'their people' taking risks
- you'll be frightened that your risk might lead to failure and sometimes you might even be scared that it might lead to success.

Every organisation has its own horror stories about risk taking and its consequences – think about it and you'll soon be able to come up with your own. Most of the time this happens because you and your co-workers aren't clear about whether taking a risk is compatible with the organisation's:

- strategic objectives
- culture, or
- attitude to risk.

The process of managing risk and overcoming these barriers to risk taking in the workplace isn't one that's quick or easy. But it is worthwhile; as John F. Kennedy told us:

'The Chinese use two brush strokes to write the word "crisis".
One brush stroke stands for danger; the other for opportunity.'

So, let's now move on to look at how the process of risk management can add to your leadership.

Can you manage risk?

When you think about the state of the world these days it's not surprising to find that the idea that you can manage risk has become increasing popular. For not only are there more risks; their consequences – potential or actual – have become more significant. As a result, organisations of all sorts and sizes face widening ranges of risks with significant potential to affect their ability to achieve their objectives. As a consequence, by the end of the twentieth century, the national standards bodies of a number of countries had created national standards designed to address the how, why and when of risk management. These included Australia (AS/NZS 4360), Canada (CAN/CSA-Q850) and Japan (JIS Q 2001). In the United Kingdom the three professional bodies of risk management practitioners produced a risk management standard that was translated into a number of European languages and adopted by the Federation of European Risk Management Associations. In the United States, the Committee of Sponsoring Organisations of the Treadway Commission (COSO) produced documents addressing the implementation of risk management within both large and small enterprises. Techniques such as Hazards and Operability studies (HAZOP) and Hazard Analysis studies (HAZAN) appeared – initially to analyse the risks and hazards of chemical process systems but later extended to other types of systems including complex operations and software systems. In 1999, the publication of the Turnbull report on Corporate Governance led the UK Government's Office of the Cabinet (OGC) to put together guidance to encourage organisations to take a sound approach to risk. This was revised in 2004 and by June 2010 the UK Financial Reporting Council had revised the UK Corporate Governance Code (see Further Information and Reading) to state that companies should *'maintain sound risk management and internal control systems'*.

The release – in late 2009 – of the first international risk management standard, *ISO 31000:2009 Risk Management – Principles and Guidelines (ISO 31000)*, represented a 'quantum leap' forward in the journey towards the creation of a standard approach to risk management. This standard describes a risk management platform that can be used to manage risks that arise from any source – irrespective of the organisation's size, type, complexity, structure, activities or location and states that risk management is a set of *'coordinated activities to direct and control an organisation with regard to risk'*. It also turns away from the view that risk generates consequences that are exclusively negative to one that says risk can also have positive consequences.

Risk management – why?

So why do you need to manage risk and what benefits will you gain by doing so? You'll find the answer to this question when you take a look at the aims and objectives that lie behind the process of risk management. These tell you that the aim of risk management is to help you, as a leader, achieve your vision by first identifying the risks, and then choosing the right response to the threats and opportunities that are created by uncertainty. Doing this – managing your risks – has some quite considerable benefits. These include:

- fewer shocks, unwelcome surprises and 'banana skins'
- better identification of new opportunities
- support of strategic and business planning
- a response to risk that's proactive rather than reactive
- more effective use of resources and better project management
- better contingency planning
- protection of organisation reputation and stakeholder confidence.

But getting to these benefits of risk management isn't a one–off exercise. For risk management that's really effective is a process that's:

- integrated into the organisation's processes – including its decision-taking system
- systematic, structured, timely, transparent and inclusive, and
- responsive to change and capable of continual improvement.

Getting to this point – to where you've got an effective risk management system – doesn't happen overnight. It takes real effort, the support of senior management, and the commitment and support of all involved. But once you've got there you'll start to reap the sort of benefits listed above. You'll do that because you've got the sort of risk management system that's been set up and operates in the ways that are described in the following sections.

Risk management – how do you set it up?

When you take a look at ISO 31000 you'll see that the steps that need to be taken towards getting your risk management system set up are really quite clear. You'll see that, initially, you'll need to identify the environment in which your risk management system will be running. You'll do this because you need to be aware of the nature and limits of your organisation's risk appetite and risk management activities. This environment has two aspects – external and internal. For example, you'll need to consider the external aspects of the environment in which the organisation operates – such as its social, cultural, political and economic dimensions – and the alignment of these with internal factors such as strategy, resources and capabilities. As you saw earlier in this book (Chapter 3 – Who's got the map?), tools such as Strengths, Weaknesses, Opportunities, and Threats (SWOT) and Political, Economic, Social, Technological, Legal and Environmental (PESTLE) analysis can be used to explore both of these dimensions using the factors listed in Table 6.2 on page 110.

Next, you'll need to generate a risk management policy. This should identify the organisation's objectives for its risk management process and the links between that policy and the processes used to manage the organisation's movement towards its strategic objectives. This policy should also clearly state things like:

- who's accountable for managing risk
- how conflicting interests are dealt with
- the organisation's level of risk appetite or risk aversion
- processes, methods and tools that will be used

Table 6.2: Context factors (Source: ISO 31000)

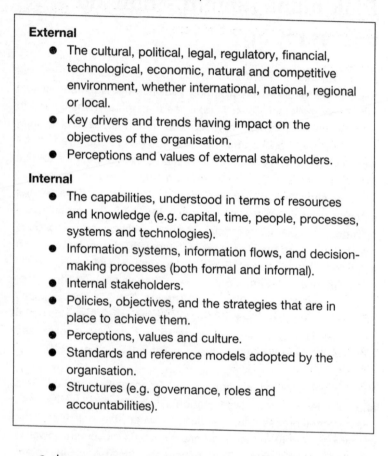

External
- The cultural, political, legal, regulatory, financial, technological, economic, natural and competitive environment, whether international, national, regional or local.
- Key drivers and trends having impact on the objectives of the organisation.
- Perceptions and values of external stakeholders.

Internal
- The capabilities, understood in terms of resources and knowledge (e.g. capital, time, people, processes, systems and technologies).
- Information systems, information flows, and decision-making processes (both formal and informal).
- Internal stakeholders.
- Policies, objectives, and the strategies that are in place to achieve them.
- Perceptions, values and culture.
- Standards and reference models adopted by the organisation.
- Structures (e.g. governance, roles and accountabilities).

- how resources needed for the risk management process will be provided and what they are
- the ways of measuring and reporting risk management performance
- what provision is made for periodic review and verification of the risk management policy and process
- need for continuous improvement.

As a part of this you'll need to assemble a package of tools and processes that you can use to identify, analyse and evaluate risks and Table 6.3 identifies some of these.

Table 6.3: Risk management tools

- Brainstorming
- Questionnaires
- Industry benchmarking
- Scenario analysis
- Risk assessment workshops
- Incident and accident investigation
- HAZOP (Hazard & Operability Studies)
- Market surveys
- Test marketing
- Research and development
- Business impact analysis
- Dependency modelling
- SWOT analysis (Strengths, Weaknesses, Opportunities, Threats)
- Event tree analysis
- Real Option Modelling
- Statistical inference
- PESTLE analysis (Political, Economic, Social, Technical, Legal, Environmental)
- Threat analysis
- Fault tree analysis
- FMEA (Failure Mode & Effect Analysis)

Existing management controls should also be assessed in terms of both their risk level and their potential use as a risk assessment tool.

In addition to doing all of these things you'll also need to make sure that you've got the 'right' systems at the core of your risk management process.

Risk management – the core process

If your risk management process is going to work you'll need to be absolutely sure that, at its core, there lies a simple but effective four-step process:

1. Identify the risk
2. Analyse the risk
3. Evaluate the risk
4. Treat or do something about the risk.

Let's look at these in more detail.

Risk identification

This initial step sets out to generate a list of risks based on those events that might affect your organisation's ability to achieve your vision. It's vital that you make sure that this list is as comprehensive as possible. Miss off a risk and it won't get included in the later analysis that leads to the answers to the 'what do we do about this risk?' question. Obvious candidates for this list include those risks that contain the potential to enhance, prevent, degrade or delay your organisation's achievement of its vision. But it's also important that you include the risks associated with not pursuing an opportunity as well as the risks whose source is outside the control of the organisation.

To do this you'll need to have a good knowledge of a wide range of things – such as the culture and history of your organisation, the market in which it operates, the legal, social, political and cultural environment in which it exists, as well as its strategic objectives.

You may also need to classify these risks using, for example, the following headings:

- **Strategic risks** – about the long-term strategic objectives of the organisation, such as capital availability, political risks, changes in regulations and laws and changes in the physical environment.
- **Operational risks** – about day-to-day issues such as machines breaking down or factory fires.
- **Financial risks** – about the management and control of your organisation's finances and the effects of factors such as availability of credit, foreign exchange rates and interest rates.
- **Knowledge management** – about knowledge resources such as copyright and patents and the experience and knowledge of key staff.
- **Compliance** – about issues such as health and safety, environmental, trade descriptions, consumer protection and data protection.

Risk analysis

Once you've identified your risk and got a 'bare bones' or outline description of it, you're going, in this next step, to put some flesh on those bones. You'll need to do it methodically and thoroughly by using the risk identification tools and techniques identified in Table 6.3 and by making sure that you've got relevant and up-to-date information. The outcome of your work will, of course, be about things like the probability of your risk occurring and the possible consequences of that risk. Often it's enough to rate these in relative – rather than absolute – terms as you'll see in Tables 6.4 and 6.5 and Figure 6.1.

Table 6.4: Occurrence rating

Estimation	Description	Symptoms
Probable	Likely to occur each year or > 25% chance	Could occur several times within 5 years
Possible	Likely to occur within 5-year period or < 25% chance	Could occur once within 5-year period
Remote	Not likely within 5-year period or < 2% chance	Hasn't happened yet

Table 6.5: Consequence rating

High	Significant impact on organisation's finances, strategy or operations. High level of stakeholder concern.
Medium	Moderate impact on organisation's finances, strategy or operations. Moderate level of stakeholder concern.
Low	Low impact on organisation's finances, strategy or operations. Little or no stakeholder concern.

Project change process

	Been done before	Never been done before
Project outcome		
Been done before	Low Risk	Medium Risk
Never been done before	Medium Risk	High Risk

Figure 6.1: Project risk matrix

Risk evaluation

The purpose of risk evaluation is that of assisting you to make a decision about what you're going to do about the risk that you're looking at. You'll do that by using the outcomes of the risk analysis you undertook in the previous step and comparing those to the risk criteria that your organisation has established. These risk criteria may be complex, involving factors such as costs and benefits, legal requirements, environmental factors and concerns of stakeholders. The outcome of this step is information that's designed to help you to make a decision – about what you're going to do next.

Risk treatment

This is where you make your decision. You'll face three alternatives and these will tell you that you can:

- accept the risk as it is, or
- modify or treat the risk in order to make it tolerable, or
- avoid it all together by not moving forward in the way that you'd planned to.

The first and the last of these alternatives are quite straightforward – you either do or don't do what you'd planned to do and, as a consequence, do or don't accept the risk. The modification or treatment alternative is, however, slightly more complicated. It's often a cyclical process in which you assess the results of an initial risk treatment and then decide whether the resultant risk levels are tolerable. If they're not tolerable you'll then generate a new risk treatment and then assess the effect of that treatment. This will go on until the treated risk reached complies with your organisation's risk criteria.

During this process you'll continue to face choices about what you do.

For you can:

- avoid the risk by not starting or not continuing with the modified activity that gave rise to it
- remove the source of the risk or reduce its effects
- reduce the likelihood of the risk happening
- change or reduce the effect of the consequences
- share the risk with someone else, or
- do it, i.e. accept the modified risk.

You might want to combine these treatments by, for example, reducing the likelihood of the risk happening as well as changing the consequences. Whatever you do you need to be aware that the risk treatment that you choose can itself introduce risks. These also need to be analysed, evaluated and treated.

Risk management – how do we make it work?

Now that you've looked at the process of risk management you're ready to move on to the next step – that of bringing that risk management process to life. Doing this starts with a simple and straightforward step – that is that you have to make sure that it's understood by all who will use it.

But doing this isn't an overnight process. It takes training, communication and practice and those take planning and resources. Once it's completed, you're ready for the next step – that of starting to use your risk management process and making sure that you keep on using it. Doing that means that you'll monitor and review the process mechanism and its outcomes. Hopefully you'll get confirmation that the various risk management elements and activities are actually working effectively. If you don't, any gaps or faults that are identified need to be sorted out. But even if your risk management process is working well you'll still need to 'tweak' and enhance its key elements in order to improve its performance. Doing all this and doing it well means that your risk management process will do what it's supposed to do – it'll continuously, systematically and proportionally address the risks surrounding your organisation's activities.

Doing all of this and doing it well will also have significant side effects – it will change the way that your organisation's management and staff carry out their duties and communicate with each other. It will also affect both the content and manner of your organisation's communications with its shareholders, customers and other stakeholders. In short, it will change the culture of your organisation and that will change the way that you lead.

Chapter checklist

In this chapter you've taken a look at risk and how it can be managed. Use the list below to check where you've got to. If you've missed something or don't understand it go back to the page given and read through it again.

- Human beings and risk have been together for a long, long time – and will probably continue to do so into the distant future (page 101).
- You'll find risk everywhere (page 102).
- Risk is always associated with a potential future action and shifted from the abstract to the real when a decision is taken (page 102).
- The word 'risk' has had varied history that has taken it from 'seeking prosperity' through 'something bad could happen here' to the 'effect of uncertainty on objectives' (page 103).
- Being a leader is a risky business – wherever you do it (page 105).
- There have been several standards for the process of risk management (page 106).
- The current international standard for risk management is ISO 31000:2009 (page 107).
- Risk management aims to help organisations to achieve their vision by identifying risks and then choosing the right response to those risks (page 108).
- Effective risk management is:
  - integrated into the organisation's processes
  - systematic, structured, timely, transparent and inclusive
  - responsive to change and capable of continual improvement (page 108).

- An effective risk management system needs to be set up carefully and thoroughly and should include a clear risk management policy statement, a package of risk management tools and a good understanding of the context in which it is operating (page 110).
- The core process of risk management has four key steps:
  - risk identification
  - risk analysis
  - risk evaluation
  - risk treatment (pages 112–116).
- Shifting your risk management process to the point where it makes a valuable contribution to your organisation's well-being needs you to:
  - train your people
  - communicate with them
  - give them the space to practise their risk management (page 117).
- An effective risk management system will change not only your organisation's culture but also the way that you lead (page 117).

Skills checkout

Doing, rather than just reading about, the things in this chapter will be another demanding but worthwhile task. It'll need you to continue to develop, refine and expand your individual 'bundle' of skills. If you think about what you've read you soon realise that these will include skills such as:

analysing	risk assessment
planning	risk management
influencing and persuading	involving others
communicating	decision making
prioritising	consulting

monitoring
scenario building
reviewing
contingency planning

thinking systematically
evaluating
managing and presenting
information

All of these are needed for Unit B10 of the Providing Direction section of the UK National Occupational Standards for Management and Leadership.

07

Can you hear me?

Communicating well is an absolute must if you're going to make things happen as a leader. In this chapter you'll look at the how, why and when of making sure that your communications 'hit the spot'. You'll get a sense of the framework of those communications and the benefits of making sure that they are effective. You'll also look at the factors that, if you let them, will limit your ability to communicate with other people. By the end of this chapter you'll also have a good understanding of the strengths and weaknesses of your written, spoken and bodily communication.

The beginning

Leaders – as you'll see in Lord Bichard's interview at the end of this book – get things done through people. But this doesn't happen because of the great reports, memos or emails that they write or even the speeches that they make – it happens because of the live conversations that they have with other people.

But, you may say, that's something that we all do. Having a conversation is a day-by-day, hour-by-hour, minute-by-minute event – wherever you are and whoever you're with. But the reality is that most of us don't do this well. There's lots of evidence – from research and our own experience – that tells us that we rarely put enough thought, care or effort into what we say and we hardly ever listen to what is said to us with enough skill to ensure that we *really* understand what's being said. All of this leads to misunderstandings and mistakes and those, in their turn, lead to arguments, altercations, quarrels, rows and even lovers' tiffs.

Here's just one example:

The new employee stood before the paper shredder looking confused.

'Need any help?' a secretary asked.

'Yes,' he replied. 'How does this thing work?'

'Simple,' she said, taking the fat report from his hand and feeding it into the shredder.

'Thanks,' he said, '– but where do the copies come out?'

One of the reasons for all of this miscommunication is the fact that communication is a skill or competence in which few of us are formally trained. Sure, we're all taught how to talk, read and write, but we're rarely taught how to use these skills in ways that lead to communication that's effective. Yet our lives abound with situations that cry out for and even demand effective communication. In the marketplace, the boardroom, the workshop and even in the bedroom, communication is *the* pivotal skill. It's also a skill that's an absolute must if you're going to succeed in leading people.

What's it all about?

If you look up the word 'communication' in your average dictionary you'll find that it tells you that it's a word that's about the *'imparting, conveying, or exchange of ideas, knowledge and information'*. It might even go on to suggest that you use 'speech, writing, or signs' to carry out your communication. However, when you take time out to think about this definition and compare it to your own experience you'll find that it falls short of what happens in the real world. For most communication goes well beyond just exchanging 'ideas, knowledge and information'. It's a core skill when it comes to the way that we interact with each other. We use it, for example, to express praise or love or hate; we also use it when we need to tell others about our anger, sadness, pain and pleasure. It's key to our social relationships. Add it all up and you'll find that the 'bandwidth' of communication encompasses:

- data or information
- sentiments, feelings and emotions
- standards, values and beliefs, and
- opinions, hypotheses, ideas and notions.

This communication can also take place in all sort of situations, such as:

- when you talk or write to one other person
- when you address a group, crowd or audience
- within a group with several people talking to each other, and
- when a group of people interacts with another group.

Communication takes place around us all the time. As a leader you're going to be immersed in it and you're going to have to make sure that your communications *really* work. You'll take the first step towards that in the next section where you'll take a look at the ways and means of your communication.

Ways and means

There are three ways that we use to communicate and all of them involve the use of a language in one form or another. For you can:

- **speak to** or talk with another person – using the spoken words of your chosen language
- **write to** another person – using the written words of your chosen language
- **use body language** in the form of gestures, facial expressions and touch.

You'll have noticed by now that only two of these – speaking and writing – are the subjects of any sort of formal teaching. Our parents teach us to speak and our parents and our schools teach us about writing and the associated act of reading. As a consequence, it's often assumed that you only need to take into account the spoken or the written modes when you're thinking or talking about communication.

But that's not only inaccurate, it's also unrealistic.

For the communication that flows between us all encompasses much more than just the words we write or speak. Here's an example: you're in a conversation with someone – you're standing together and because of that you can easily see and hear each other. You know what you want to say and you've thought through how you're going to say it.

So all you have to do is say the words, right?

Well, no, that isn't all you have to do.

For when you speak, the tone of your voice will be part of the message that you send. As you can see and are close to the person, the gestures you use, your movements and use of space, whether you do or don't touch the other person and your facial expressions will all add to, complement or even, sometimes, contradict the message contained in the words that you speak.

So your communication isn't just about words.

In fact, research suggests that, in a conversation like this, as little as 10 per cent of the total message you send lies in the words you use. The other 90 or so per cent of your message involves the way you say those words and, most of all, the 'language' of your body. This 'body language' is just as eloquent as your words and it's often used, usually unconsciously, to communicate about things like feelings, like/dislike, power, status and responsiveness. You'll come back to look at 'body language' in more detail later in this chapter. But, before you do that, there's something important that you need to look at.

One way or two way?

Another outcome of the 'speaking and writing only' view of communications is the idea that our communications are one-way messages – you tell somebody something and that's it.

Again, that's not only inaccurate, it's also unrealistic and, even worse, it's ineffective.

For all your communications – however they are undertaken – are two-way. The other side of this two-way process is called feedback. Even when you're issuing instructions or telling someone where to go, the person that you're talking to is giving you feedback. But this feedback doesn't have to be in the form of words – it can be contained in the expression on their face, whether they are looking at you or the way they are standing. All of these will tell you whether your message has been heard and understood and, if you're 'tuned-in' enough to read it, how the listener feels about you and your message (see Figure 7.1).

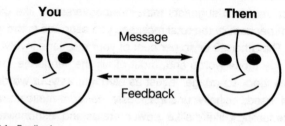

Figure 7.1: Feedback

But, despite the fact that it's 'two-way', this sort of communication has its limitations and, because of that, is often called *'partial communication'*. If you're really going to be an effective leader then this feedback needs to change. For it needs to move up, upgrade, to where it's more than a mere acknowledgement of a message received; it needs to change until this feedback contains as much information as the original message.

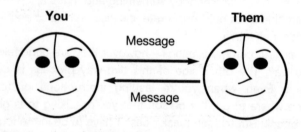

Figure 7.2: Full communication

When this happens you'll find that you've shifted up into what's called *full communication* (see Figure 7.2). Here the roles (of speaker and listener) alternate and overlap and, when they do that, they both convey the full range of information, ideas and feelings. This level of communication is a vital ingredient to the process of leading people. It will happen when you and the people you're communicating with have:

- shared concerns, objectives and targets
- adequate trust in each other, and
- are both committed to achieving an outcome that's mutually acceptable.

But that's not all that you need to achieve if you are going to communicate successfully – you'll also need to make sure that your communication has a purpose, objective or desired outcome. In other words, you need to have a reason for doing it.

Purposes, objectives and outcomes

At a first glance, it would seem that there are, potentially, millions and millions of reasons for your communications. But, as a leader, the reality is that your communication, at its core, takes place for a single reason. This is that you want to reach out to people and affect the ways in which they:

- think and feel about things, and/or
- do things.

Each time that you communicate the detail will vary. But the core reason will remain the same. The 'doing' verbs commonly associated with all of this include:

- instructing
- influencing, and
- exchanging information.

You can, of course, combine all of these together. However, if your communication is going to be effective then you'll have to decide and then make clear which of these is your main objective.

But that's not the only thing that you need to do if you're going to be a communicative leader – you're also going to have to learn to listen.

Listening

Learning to listen to what's said, rather than just hearing it, is a vital skill for a leader. The benefits of doing this are considerable. Listening gives you access to valuable facts, opinions and information as well as gaining you the respect and co-operation of your co-workers. Being able to listen carefully and effectively will get you to where you:

- are able to build a better rapport with co-workers and clients – and, as a consequence, have better relationships with them
- are more effective in a team-based environment because you've a better understanding of co-workers
- are better able to understand the other's point of view and, as a result, are better at resolving problems
- are more aware of the underlying meanings in what others say and consequently act less defensively and more encouragingly.

All of this means that you'll be able to take better decisions and will be better able to understand what is expected of you in your journey towards your vision.

So, now that you're clear about the benefits of the chosen, deliberate action of listening how do you get to the point where you can do it?

Effective listening – steps and stages

The process of becoming an effective listener starts with an automatic, reflexive act – that of hearing. To hear well you need to:

- make sure that your hearing is OK – if you're not sure, get it checked by a doctor or an audiologist
- position yourself to hear – face the person that you're talking to
- turn off or reduce background noise and distractions – switch off your mobile phone, close the office door
- choose quiet settings – choose a place to talk that's away from noisy areas.

But effective listening isn't just about hearing the words that people say. Studies of spoken and line-of-sight workplace communication tell us that:

- less than one-tenth of the message is provided by the words spoken
- around four-tenths of the message comes from the way those words are spoken, and
- the remaining half of the message is provided by body language – such as facial expressions, posture, gestures, eye contact.

Even when you can't see the person that you're talking to (as in a telephone conversation) there's a lot more information coming your way than just mere words. To catch that extra information you'll have listen for:

- the emphasis that's placed on some words

- the pauses between the words or sentences
- the pitch, stress and volume of these words or sentences.

If you're going to become an effective listener then you're going to have to acquire, practise and use a unique package of skills. These are the skills of attending, following and reflecting; skills that you'll find out more about when you read *Instant Manager: Successful Workplace Communication* (see Further Information and Reading).

Acquiring these skills isn't an overnight event. It'll take time and practice for you to hone and polish the how and when of their use. But making this commitment – to effective listening – is worthwhile. Use Table 7.1 as a checklist for your listening.

Table 7.1: A guide to good listening

---

1. **Indicate by your manner that what is being said is being absorbed:**
   - Look, encourage by nodding, and reinforce – *'I see'*.

2. **Avoid self/others interrupting:**
   - Don't interrupt, unless it is to ask for clarification.
   - Stop or avoid others interrupting.

3. **Resist distractions:**
   - Listen for the theme of the message.
   - Focus on what the speaker is saying.
   - Avoid verbal, visual or physical distractions.

4. **Don't judge content or delivery:**
   - Concentrate on listening without judging.

5. **Avoid daydreaming:**
   - Make yourself listen, don't tune out.
   - Maintain eye contact, lean forward, occasionally summarise – *'So you are saying …'*.

---

6. **Let him or her talk:**
   - Don't rush to fill the speaker's pauses.
   - If they stop, encourage them to continue – *'Go on'* or *'What happened then?'*

7. **Keep your mind open:**
   - Listen in an understanding way.
   - Don't prejudge what they will say before they've said it!

8. **Listen between the words:**
   - Be alert for omissions, sometimes the essential message is contained in what is *not* said.
   - Listen for feeling as well as meaning.
   - Ask yourself is the speaker: critical or neutral?; optimistic or pessimistic?; confident or defensive?; open or evasive?

9. **Check your interpretation of the speaker's message:**
   - Clarify by: *'So the situation is …?'* or *'Do you mean …?'*
   - Ask questions if you don't understand.
   - Ask yourself: *'Do I really know what they are saying?'*

Bodily communication

You've already seen that body language is extraordinarily important to the ways and means of your communication. This sort of communication has been with humankind for a long time – there even seems to be some evidence that using your body to communicate is an innate or 'hard wired' potentiality for us all. As a result, when you use non-verbal communication, a number of things happen – though not all of them come about because of a conscious choice on your part. Non-verbal or bodily communication enables you to:

- overcome the limitations that words sometimes have – as, for example, when explaining shapes or indicating directions
- gain an additional and separate communication channel that allows you to expand the complexity or meaning of a verbal message.

But those aren't the only things that happen when you use body language. For when you do that, you also:

- hint at, signal or even express your inner feelings
- give messages that are often seen to be more genuine than your spoken messages
- often express or hint at feelings that are inappropriate to the place or situation that you're in – that are beyond the boundaries of 'social etiquette'.

When you think about all this you'll soon realise that the power and effects of your body language are considerable. However, this language of movement, gesture and facial expression is one that you are usually more aware of in others (though often unconsciously so) than in yourself. As a leader, however, you'll need to change that situation – so that you're able to both 'speak' and 'read' body language.

Body language – the ways and means

You've already seen that in a face-to-face conversation you can use bodily communication for all sorts of things. You can, for example:

- repeat what's been said – as in saying 'that way' and pointing

- contradict what's been said – as in saying 'I'm happy' without a smile
- use gestures as a substitute for words – as in shaking your head to say 'no'
- complement words – as in saying 'I'm happy' and smiling
- regulate conversations by nods, eye movements and posture shifts.

As you would imagine, all of this has been the subject of considerable research and we'll now take a brief look at some of the more common forms of bodily communication. You'll find more information on these and other aspects of body language in *Instant Manager: Body Language* and *Instant Manager: Successful Workplace Communication* (see Further Information and Reading).

Gestures

Gestures get used a lot to send a visual signal. This can be deliberate – as in a wave of recognition – or incidental – as in the hand movements associated with a sneeze – or unconscious – as when you scratch your head when thinking about something. Sometimes these gestures have a direct verbal equivalent and get used in situations where:

- verbal communication is difficult , or
- speed or privacy or visibility over a distance are needed.

But gestures can also be used to illustrate, repeat, complement or underline the spoken word – as when you point or beckon, describe a shape in space or make movements about 'up' or 'around'.

You'll also use gestures in your conversations – in order, for example, to show your interest in what's being said or to signal that you want to say something. Gestures that are unconscious are often called 'leakage' gestures because they display or hint at your hidden feelings, thoughts and emotions. These will occur despite your best efforts to control them and despite the pressure of social 'rules' about controlling your gestures or expressing emotions. Simple examples include touching your body, when under stress, in ways that replicate or mimic the actions of others when comforting you – such as hugging yourself or covering your mouth with a hand when wishing to mislead or deceive others.

Facial expressions

We all read faces. It's such a common thing for us to do that we often don't realise that we're doing it. And, of course, other people read our faces. Your expressions are rich in information about your thoughts, feelings and intentions. Like your gestures, these facial expressions can be deliberate – as with the polite 'social' smile – or incidental – as when you screw your eyes up in bright sunlight – or unconscious – as when you are genuinely surprised, shocked or alarmed.

In social situations your facial expressions are observed closely by others and can provide considerable information about what you are thinking and feeling. However, some of these expressions – such as a smile, a laugh or a frown – can be very easily faked. Nevertheless, other facial expressions – such as those involving small movements of your lip and jaw muscles and the muscles around your eyes – are much more difficult to fake and do provide clues about genuine, rather than pretended, feelings.

Gaze

When you gaze at someone you look at them in a steady or fixed way. This gazing can be done for a short or a long time, by one person or both and can take place while talking or listening. It can also be expressive, direct or indirect and can generate a wide range of responses on the part of the 'gazed–at' person. In most social situations, however, your gazing will be limited by social rules or norms – 'it's not polite to stare'. As a result, your social gazing is discontinuous and involves glances of a limited duration. Nevertheless, even small changes in this sort of gazing will often signal things like the desire to start or finish a conversation. This happens because you look at those you wish to communicate with and generally do so before you start to speak. You also, when speaking, will glance at people in order to confirm their attention or to underline or emphasise what is being said. Using gaze to communicate with those around you is a common and well-used pattern of behaviour, despite the fact that the rules of gaze are complex and sometimes misunderstood or misinterpreted.

Touch

Almost all of your workplace touching will be social in nature. As such, it will include such actions as:

- greeting people by shaking hands or embracing
- influencing people by touching their arm, hand or shoulder whilst speaking
- directing or guiding people by a light clasp on the arm or a slight touch to the back.

There are many variations of these basic forms of social touching; variations that reflect the nature and intimacy of the relationship between the toucher and the touched. For example, touch initiated by high status individuals in the workplace is more likely to be an expression of dominance than an expression of affection. But touch in the workplace does have its downside as it can be associated with sexual harassment. The level and type of social touching that is acceptable differs between cultures. For example, Arab, South American and Southern European cultures are often seen as 'contact' cultures while Japanese, British and North American cultures are seen as 'non or low contact' cultures.

Posture

The ways that you stand, sit, recline, lean, place or cross your arms and lower or tilt your head all come together to make up what is called your 'posture'. This posture will often reveal much about how you feel about others. For example, if you see that someone is sitting stiffly or rigidly this could indicate that person is tense or with someone they dislike or fear. But the posture that you adopt doesn't just tell others about how you feel, it can also work the other way – to induce an emotion in you. For example, research tells us that when people sit in a slumped, head-down, depressed position they appear to develop feelings of helplessness more readily than when they sit in an expansive, upright posture.

But the postures that you adopt are not only an expression of how you feel; they are also often the postures that are approved for that situation by the 'culture' in which you live or work. There are, for example, 'correct' postures for eating, giving a lecture or presentation, being interviewed, sunbathing and riding a horse. If you don't adopt the 'correct' posture then you may be seen as 'uncivilised' or 'eccentric'. Posture is also used differently by men and women – men, for example, usually sit with knees and ankles apart while women sit with knees and ankles together or only slightly apart. But posture on its own will rarely tell you all that you need to know about what people are thinking or feeling. Nevertheless, when taken with other signals such as facial expression and gesture, it can provide a rich source of information.

Appearance

Your appearance is a rich and complex mix of many factors. Your height and build, whether you do or don't wear make-up, your hair, hands, overall fitness, whether you have a tattoo or pierced ears and what sort of clothes and jewellery or badges you wear – all of these and many other factors blend together to create your individual appearance. This appearance is important. For studies tell us that people make judgements about you and your character from the way that you appear to them. They usually do this very quickly – within the first ten seconds of meeting you!

Your appearance – or the way that you appear to others – can, for example:

- tell them about your chosen 'self image', or
- tell them whether you're a member of a club or organisation, or
- tell them what your job is.

As you've already seen a lot of factors play a major role in your appearance. They give signals about your personality, social status, attitude towards others, whether you are, or aren't, sexually available and whether you are, or aren't, concerned about what's 'fashionable'. Most of the time you'll conform to what's 'normal' for a given situation. For example, you'll wear a suit for a job interview and a dinner jacket or formal dress for a formal dinner. But your appearance is actually quite flexible. You can, for example, easily change the way that you dress. You can also change the shape of your nose or face and remove some signs of ageing by having plastic surgery. Whatever your chosen appearance might be, it's done with a purpose: that of influencing the impressions or perceptions that others have about you. For people will often adjust how they behave towards you based on how they see you.

Now, finally, you're going to take a brief look at the ways in which you use the spoken and the written word to communicate. You'll find a lot more detail on how to use these in the workplace – as when you negotiate, do presentations, explain and persuade – in *Instant Manager: Successful Workplace Communication* and *Instant Manager: Effective Presenting* (see Further Information and Reading).

The spoken word

Speech – particularly line-of-sight one-to-one speech – is the most direct form of communication. It's also the most flexible of the ways that you'll use to communicate – you can speak formally, informally, at length, briefly, emotionally or coolly. You can use the spoken word in conversations, speeches, presentations, telephone calls and video links and you can use it when you or the person you're speaking to can, or can't, see one another. The spoken word will make a major contribution to your leading as its use can:

- make people feel that they have been personally consulted
- lead to expression of feelings as well as ideas
- enable sharing and comparing
- facilitate immediate feedback, and
- complement non-verbal communication when face to face.

The written word

The written word is indirect in nature and once created is fixed in its form and content. Using it, however, does mean that you're able to express your own ideas and feelings without having to respond to or cope with the other person's reactions and responses. This indirectness also helps you to choose the 'right' words and to edit and reshape your message until it is satisfactory. A written communication can be brief or lengthy and formal or informal. It can also reflect your personal style. Organisations often have 'rules' about the style and presentation of written material. The tangible form of written communication means that it can:

- be easily copied and so provide physical evidence of transmission and content
- be sent to a number of people at the same time.

Communication – do's and don'ts

As you approach the end of this chapter it's worth reflecting that, so far, you've taken a pretty broad, but comprehensive, 'glance' at the how's of communication. But if you're going to ensure that all of this makes a positive contribution to your leadership then there are two factors that need to be emphasised. These will tell you that, however you do it, your communication will only be successful if you are clear about:

- what you want to achieve by your communication
- who you're going to communicate with
- where and how you're going to communicate.

These mean that you're going to have to think about things like the nature of the message (formal, informal, confidential, etc.), who it's going to (shareholders, the project team, the machine shop, etc.), what communication channels are available and their cost (meetings, letters, telephone calls, faxes, conference calls) and your need to record the content of the message or the response it generates.

But despite your decisions on all of these factors you may still find that your communication isn't successful. This can happen because of environmental factors such as distractions and noise, transmission faults – as when your message is sent in a way that's inappropriate or contains jargon or inappropriate language and creates perception and attitude problems. These might include messages based on false or incorrect assumptions or messages in which the sender uses a word in one context or with one meaning while the receiver uses the same word in a different context or with a different meaning. Anticipating and bypassing these limiting factors is a key issue when it comes to leadership. Do that and communicate with care and forethought and you'll soon begin to reap the benefits of effective communication. Don't do it – and become a careless communicator – and you'll find that your attempts to gain success in your leading are frustrated by misunderstanding, misinterpretation and confusion.

Chapter checklist

In this chapter you've taken a look at the how, why and when of your leadership communication. Use the list below to check where you've got to. If you've missed something or don't understand it go back to the page given and read through it again.

- Communication is a skill that's key to the process of leading people (page 122).
- Communication takes place when you:
  - **speak** with or talk to another person – using the spoken words of your chosen language
  - **write** to another person – again using the written words of your chosen language
  - **use body language** in the form of gestures, facial expressions and touch (page 124).

- All communication involves feedback (page 125).
- Partial communication involves limited feedback and full communication involves total feedback (page 126).
- As a leader your communication will be about reaching out to people and affecting the ways in which they:
  - think and feel about things and/or
  - do things (page 127).
- Listening, rather than just hearing, is a vital skill for a leader (page 128).
- Listening involves attending, reflecting and following (page 130).
- Bodily communication involves gestures, facial expressions, gaze, touch, posture and appearance (pages 133–137).
- The spoken word is the most direct and flexible form of communication whereas the written word is indirect in nature and once created is fixed in its form and content (page 138).
- Successful communication happens when you are clear about the objective, with whom, where and how of your communication and when you anticipate and bypass the factors that will limit the quality of that communication (page 139).

Skills checkout

Doing, rather than just reading about, the things that you've been reading about in this chapter will be another demanding but worthwhile task. It'll need you to continue to develop, refine and expand your individual 'bundle' of skills. If you think about what you've read you soon realise that these will include skills such as:

analysing	communicating
influencing and persuading	setting objectives
information management	presenting information
involving others	obtaining/providing feedback
motivating	valuing and supporting
inspiring	consulting

Communicating and its associated skills are so important to the process of leadership that they feature in all the units of the Providing Direction section of the UK National Occupational Standards for Management and Leadership.

08

Where do you do it?

This chapter takes a look at two of the most important of the places in which your leading will get done – the organisation and the team. It looks at and compares the characteristics and demands of each of these and identifies the influences that these exert upon the process of leading.

Back to basics

If there's one thing that the proverbial 'Visitor from Mars' will talk about when they get back home, it's our organisations. The word itself – which was originally spelt as *organization* – has, according to the *Oxford English Dictionary*, its roots in biology relating to the 'development or co-ordination of parts (of the body) in order to carry out vital functions' and began to be used in the late-fifteenth century. By the late 1700s, however, its use had shifted into a social context – to describe the way in which 'particular activities or institutions are organized' and developed the alternative spelling of *organisation*.

Since then the organisation has flourished to the point where it has become an integral part of the social and economic 'bedrock' of early twenty-first century society. As a result, much has been written about organisations, resulting in a wide-ranging and substantial bibliography that draws heavily upon the disciplines of economics, psychology, sociology and systems theory. Most of this consists of attempts to explain and describe or categorise our organisations with much of its focus being upon the profit-making organisations of the world of paid work.

You've also seen (see Chapter 3 – Who's got the map?) that organisations, whatever their size, nature, history or purpose, need to be able to respond to the social, political and technical changes that push and pull at them in today's constantly changing world. This has meant that organisations have had to accept that:

- predictability and stability are things of the past
- survival demands the ability to anticipate and embrace change.

Both of these have meant that organisations have had to develop the ability to change their structures and the ways in which they operate. As a result, as you'll now see, the ways by which we describe and categorise these organisations have grown increasingly diverse.

Names and games

One of the earliest of the comments or suggestions made about the structure of organisations was that made by the Scottish writer Adam Smith (1723–90). In his now famous book *The Wealth of Nations*, Smith suggested that the division of labour could be beneficial in terms of production. One example he gave was the manufacture of pins. A single worker, he said, working on his own would probably make only 20 pins per day. However, if ten people divided up the 18 steps required to make a pin, they could make a combined amount of 48,000 pins/day. One hundred years later, the German sociologist Max Weber (1864–1920) wrote about the rational or bureaucratic organisation (see Table 8.1)

Table 8.1: The seven principles of a bureaucratic organisation

1. Business is continuous.
2. Business follows these rules:
   a. each official does certain types of work
   b. the official has the necessary authority
   c. the means of coercion available to the official are strictly limited and conditions of their use strictly defined.
3. A vertical hierarchy of authority exists with respective rights of supervision and appeal.
4. The resources necessary for the performance of assigned functions are not owned by officials – they are, however, accountable for their use.
5. Official and private business and income are separate.
6. These offices held cannot be appropriated (inherited, sold, etc.).
7. Business is conducted on the basis of written documents.

Not long after this, the American engineer Frederick Taylor (1856–1915) introduced the ideas that formed the foundation of what became known as Scientific Management. This was based on four principles:

1. Rule-of-thumb work methods should be replaced by methods based on a scientific study of the tasks.
2. Each employee should be scientifically selected, trained and developed.
3. Each worker should be given detailed instruction and supervision in the performance of their task.
4. Work should be nearly equally divided between managers and workers, so that the managers apply scientific management principles to planning the work and the workers actually perform the tasks.

All of these ideas about organisations and the ways in which they work drew heavily on the idea of the organisation as a machine that converted raw material into products and in which the worker acted as a part of the machine – a de-skilled cog.

But, by the 1920s, things had begun to change and a more human element began to enter the spectrum of views about how organisations worked. Productivity studies conducted at Western Electric's Hawthorne plant in the United States led Harvard professor Elton Mayo to conclude that workers should be viewed as members of a group rather than isolated individuals or cogs in a machine. He suggested that these informal groups exerted a strong influence on individual behaviour and said that managers must take these 'social needs' into account if they wanted to ensure that employees collaborate with – rather than work against – the organisation.

This seminal study shifted thinking about organisations into what became known as the Human Relations Movement. This focused on teams, motivation and the goals and roles of individuals within organisations – in short, on how human factors and psychology affected organisations. Eminent researchers and theoreticians included Frederick Herzberg (job enrichment and Motivator–Hygiene theory), Abraham Maslow (Hierarchy of Needs), David McClelland (Need for Achievement), and Victor Vroom (Expectancy Theory of Motivation).

However, world events, including the Second World War, shifted the emphasis back towards a more rational view of organisations involving as it did, disciplines such as operations research, large scale logistics, systems theory and rational decision theory. As a result, phrases such as bounded rationality, supply chain management (SCM) and multi-criteria decision analysis (MCDA) entered the lexicon of 'management-speak'. However, by the beginning of the twenty-first century, things had begun to change again. Ideas such as organisational ecology and the influences of anthropology, psychology and sociology were strong again. Two examples of that shift are the ideas contained in

Ricardo Semler's ideas on how to run an organisation (see Table 8.2 and Further Information and Reading) and the now classic book *Images of Organizations* written by Gareth Morgan (see Table 8.3 and Further Information and Reading).

Table 8.2: Ricardo Semler and Semco

Semco has no official structure. It has no organisational chart. There's no business plan or company strategy, no two-year or five-year plan, no goal or mission statement, no long-term budget. The company often does not have a fixed CEO. There are no vice presidents or chief officers for information technology or operations. There are no standards or practices. There's no human resources department. There are no career plans, no job descriptions or employee contracts. No one approves reports or expense accounts. Supervision or monitoring of workers is rare indeed.

Table 8.3: Images of Organization

Professor Gareth Morgan identified eight metaphors for or ways of describing organisations (see Further Information and Reading).

METAPHOR	IMPLICATIONS
Machine	A rational, logical endeavour made up of interlocking parts and structured so as to achieve predetermined outcomes with maximum efficiency.
Organism	A living organism that's born, grows, develops, declines and dies as well as adapting to a changing environment.

(Continued)

(Continued)

METAPHOR	IMPLICATIONS
Brain	Flexible, resilient and inventive endeavour with the capacity for intelligence, information processing, control and learning.
Culture	A mini-society, with its own set of distinctive values, rituals, ideologies and beliefs which form a framework for viewing and understanding events, actions and situations.
Political system	A system of political activity, with patterns of competing interests, conflict and power.
Psychic prisons	Places in which people are trapped in their own thoughts and actions and in which obsessions, mind traps, narcissism, strong emotions, illusions of control, anxieties and defence mechanisms flourish.
Flux/ transformation	Processes of transformation and change.
Instruments of domination	A system that exploits employees, the natural environment and the global economy for its own ends.

Almost all of these studies have focused on profit-making organisations. But non-profit organisations are just as significant. The range of these organisations is wide, extending as it does from those that appear, in terms of function and appearance, to be close to government agencies through to those that appear to be little more than informal networks. Nevertheless, despite all this diversity, studies tell us that many of these non-profit organisations are:

- organised
- private
- non-profit-making or distributing
- self-governing, and
- usually involve volunteer employees.

They are also as long-lived as their profit-making cousins.

Some of these non-profit-making organisations possess major economic 'clout' and others – often called non-governmental organisations (NGOs) – have become important actors on the political stage. They are also increasingly working together with their profit-making cousins. Amnesty International, for example, has worked with companies operating in zones of conflict to train business executives in human rights issues. One result of all of this is that non-profit organisations are, as one writer puts it, 'discovering management'. One example of the resulting changes has been the recent launch of a qualification for project managers working in the development sector. Developed by a consortium of 45 global agencies that share learning resources and technology, this qualification is specifically for people working in charities, humanitarian agencies and not-for-profit agencies.

But the sort of management that's needed by these non-profit organisations is different. For in many of these non-profit-making organisations the operating procedures are under the control of an executive officer while the definition and detail of the organisation's mission are in the hands of its Board. This mission is different from that of a profit-making organisation – it's almost always based on values, convictions and beliefs rather than the drive to profit. These organisations also have clients – for example, people with disabilities, children and older people – who often can't act in ways that indicate their preferences or pay for the services delivered. Nevertheless, it's reported that non-profit organisations have made their greatest 'discoveries' in the area of financial management. But whereas profit-making organisations are concerned about the management of costs and revenue for profit, the financial control exerted in non-profit-making organisations is described as being often little more than about 'cost controlling and cost cutting'.

When it comes to leading in any sort of organisation, size is also a significant factor. Sociologists tell us that as a group grows in size the number of possible person-to-person links increases rapidly. There's an equation for this; one that tells us that the number of person-to-person links (L) increases with the number of people (N) like this:

$$L = (N^2 - N) / 2$$

What this means is that in a four-member group there are six possible links; with a five-member group you have ten possible links and with a twelve-member group as many as sixty-six possible links. Life, as you know, is too short for all these links to take place. As a consequence, as a group grows in size, reaching a consensus about an issue or problem becomes increasingly difficult. As a result the need for leadership grows more evident as the group (or organisation) size increases – people have to be motivated to come together and co-operate; goals must be set; tasks assigned, scheduled, and carried out; problems solved. While in a small group these things come about because a few people trust each other and share an important purpose, large groups almost always depend on recognised leaders to manage operations.

Organisational culture

The term 'organisational culture' is used to describe the complex patterns of beliefs, values, rituals, myths and sentiments that are shared by the members of an organisation or, to put it another way, 'the way things get done around here'. This culture is significant; it influences almost everything that goes on in an organisation. It'll define, for example, the ways in which decisions get taken, how rewards are distributed, how people get treated, and, last but not least, how people are led.

One of the more accessible and easily understandable models of organisational culture was that generated by Roger Harrison (see Further Information and Reading). What he suggested was that the cultures of our organisations can be identified by where they sit on the scales of Centralisation and Formalisation (see Figure 8.1).

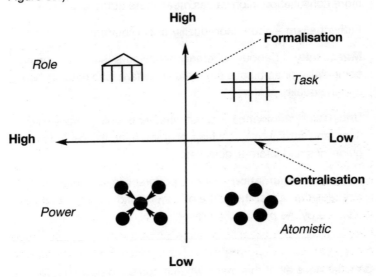

Figure 8.1: Organisational cultures

What this tells you is that a bureaucratic organisation will have a culture that rates high on both these scales while an organisation that emphasises results and getting things done (task culture) will rate high on formalisation but low on centralisation. An organisation like Ricardo Semler's Semco (see Table 8.2) will rate low on both of these scales.

But these aren't the only factors that influence an organisation's culture. Geert Hofstede indentified five factors that he used to differentiate between the cultures of different nations or countries (see Table 8.4).

Table 8.4: Geert Hofstede's cultural dimensions

Power distance – about power distribution, low values mean more consultation, high values mean more autocracy.

Individualism – about individuality or collectivism.

Masculinity – about whether behaviours such as being competitive or ambitious are more important than relationships and the quality of life.

Uncertainty avoidance – about whether people prefer explicit rules and structured activities or implicit or flexible rules or guidelines and informal activities.

Long-term orientation – about preferences for actions and attitudes that affect the future or actions and attitudes that are affected by the past or the present.

So what does all of this mean when it comes to how you do your leading in an organisation?

The first part of the answer should remind you about what you read in Chapter 2 – What's it all about? There you saw that leadership has changed and evolved to meet the demands of history and that:

- there isn't a single 'fits-all-situations' leadership style
- the style that you use will be influenced by factors related to:

- the organisation's culture, history and size
- the situation
- the followers
- the relationships that you have with them.

You also saw that, over time, leadership has become more flexible and open and with a core that's concerned with:

- future actions
- influencing people
- establishing a direction or target for these people's collective efforts
- managing these activities in line with this direction or target.

Nevertheless there are a number of core issues that you need to be aware of – whatever the nature, size or style of the organisation in which you're doing your leading.

Organisations and leading

If you get to do it, leading an organisation will be probably one of the most demanding tasks that you'll face in your working lifetime. To do it effectively, you'll have to draw on all of your experiences and skills. For example, you're going to have to articulate, explain and proselytise the vision and plan that you read about in Chapter 2 – What's it all about?, Chapter 3 – Who's got the map? and Chapter 4 – Can you see where we're going?. The range of skills that you're going to need to use to do this and all the other things associated with leading in an organisation will be considerable (see Chapter 1 – Who is this book for?, Table 1.2). But that's not all that you'll need to do. You'll also need to be able to create a sense of common purpose in your organisation – a purpose that comes from a vision that generates excitement and commitment. In doing this you'll need to take responsibility for making things happen and yet also delegate tasks to others and allow and encourage them to take decisions. In order to do all of this and do it well you'll need to be clear about your:

- own values, motivation and emotions, and
- strengths and weaknesses.

In doing these and all the other things that are needed to lead an organisation you also need to remember that, at their core, our organisations consist of people – people who, if you get your leading right, will be energetic, enthusiastic and creative – and that can't be bad.

Teams

The word 'team' gets used a lot, particularly in the workplace. When it does it's usually about the idea of several people working together in the same direction or towards the same objective. This idea of working together – in ways that are, hopefully, co-operative and harmonious – makes the idea of a team an attractive one. As a consequence the word team gets used and sometimes misused to describe the gangs, crews or groups of people that do all sorts of things and in all sorts of organisations. As a result the idea of team working has become important and the word 'team' has sprung into use all over the place. In fact, there'll probably be few of you who aren't involved in or responsible for what's described as a team.

But this idea of people working together – as a team – isn't a new one. Its earliest recorded use in the English language pre-dates the Industrial Revolution and the emergence of the corporation by a wide margin. Its strengths – and its weaknesses – were well known well before the emergence of the 'science' of management. For the team – when used well – is a powerful tool. It can make things happen. As a result, the ability to lead a team is a key skill in the workplace.

But, before you look at how you can do that, let's take a brief look at what teams do in organisations.

Teams in organisations

The sorts of tasks that teams undertake are often reflected in their titles. You'll have heard of or maybe even worked in a team such as a project team, a sales team or a management team. But that's not all that the team title can tell you. For they can also tell you something about where in the organisation the team carries out its task – as with the Computer Division management team or the Albuquerque plant safety team. Most of the teams that you'll have met in your workplace will have had such a title. This will confirm something that you already know – that out there are a huge variety of teams, teams that are doing almost anything you can think of and doing these tasks almost everywhere. But order comes to this abundance when you recognise that these teams either:

- control or run something, or
- make something, or
- do something, or
- evaluate something and make recommendations about it.

The size, composition, location and permanency of these teams is often related to what they do. An executive or management team, for example, will oversee or co-ordinate organisational activities and do that from a high position in the organisation with a small, multi-disciplined and permanent group, whereas an audit or project team will only exist until its task is complete and is usually small, consisting of people with the skills or knowledge required.

Don't forget that these teams – whatever their purpose, size or longevity – are the children of an organisation. As such they are immersed in and subject to the culture of that organisation; they are subject to its rules and procedures and influenced by its tides, rituals and seasons. All of these exert pressure on the team. The 'parent' organisation will expect the team to act in ways that are compatible with the rest of the organisation and it will also have rules – formal and informal – about how things should *not* be done. These powerful pressures can range from the subtle but insistent pressures of the organisation's culture to the need to generate quick and effective solutions to the problems that the organisation is facing – such as the need to maintain a lead position in the marketplace. They influence and in some cases define:

- what the team does, and
- the way that it does it.

For example, one organisation might only use teams to solve urgent problems – such as delays in the distribution of perishable products – while another might limit its use of teams to more general and longer-term issues – such as identifying the probable computing needs of that organisation in the mid-twenty-first century.

All of this means that, yet again, there isn't a single 'one-size-fits-all' sort of leadership for teams. It all depends – as they say – on the what, why and when of the situation that the team is operating in. Nevertheless there are some features of team leadership that are rather special.

Leadership and teams

Teams are hugely popular for a number of reasons. For the team, in all of its guises, is a device or mechanism that has the potential to enable you to:

- tap into the skills, abilities and creativity of all the people in it, and
- use all of those to greater effect in the workplace.

With a good team you can make things happen – quicker and better – and find ways of moving the pace of what happens in your workplace up a gear.

In order to do this your team will have to be:

- flexible and adaptable
- able to grow and change to meet new demands
- able to reinvent itself when individuals move on
- independent of the skills and abilities of any one member.

In short, your team has to become a group of people who work together towards a shared and meaningful outcome in ways that combine their individual skills.

Studies of teams like this tell us that their members are:

- loyal to each other and the team
- able to identify and agree a collective outcome
- keen to co-operate and collaborate together in order to achieve that outcome
- focused towards creating team – rather than individual – outcomes or 'products', and
- able to define these outcomes in ways that are specific, tangible, measurable and meaningful to all team members.

You've probably recognised by now that a team like this isn't just unusual – it's also rather special. But a team like this doesn't 'pop' into existence overnight – you have to work at it, create it, maintain and sustain it. It will need support and understanding from its parent organisation, time to grow and develop. It will also need to be given a high degree of autonomy and allowed to develop confidence that its success will be both recognised and rewarded. It acts as a lens (see Figure 8.2) bringing together and focusing all of the skills and abilities of the people who are a part of that team.

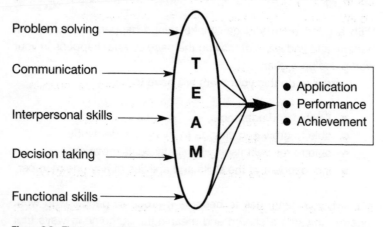

Figure 8.2: The team as a lens

In this sort of team things are different; for it has:

- a facilitator/coach rather than a leader
- goals that are set by its members rather than a leader or the parent organisation
- communication patterns that flow up *and* down
- members that:
  - take decisions together
  - work together co-operatively
  - are jointly responsible for outcomes.

A team like this needs the right 'mix' of people and one of the ways that you can make sure that this happens is to use one of the commercial self-assessment questionnaires that are available. These are based on the Belbin and the Margerison–McCann approaches to team building and the Management Team Role Indicator developed by S.P. Myers (see Further Information and Reading).

What all of this should tell you is that leading a team is different from leading an organisation. This is because the 'old' models of the team leader role – with the leader being a pivotal role at the centre of a group – won't work any more. As is so with their counterparts in organisations, the 'new' team leaders:

- co-ordinate
- guide and advise
- create an 'umbrella' under which the team can operate
- fight to get adequate resources for the team
- coach, encourage and develop team members
- act as a problem-solving resource
- recognise and acknowledge good work
- provide an example of 'how things ought to be done'.

In some teams the leadership role is mobile. It becomes one that:

- is carried by different team members – for different tasks or parts of a task
- is carried by different team members at different times in the team's development.

What all this means is that whether you do – or don't – become a team leader will depend upon a number of things, such as:

- whether your organisation can tolerate a real – rather than a partial or make-believe – team
- your skills and abilities, and
- your ability to play 'pass-the-parcel' with the team role.

Chapter checklist

In this chapter you've taken a look at two of the places in which your leading will get done – the organisation and the team. You've examined the characteristics and demands of each of these and the influences that these exert upon the process of leading. Use the list below to check where you've got to. If you've missed something or don't understand it go back to the page given and read through it again:

- The organisation has become an integral part of the social and economic 'bedrock' of early-twenty-first century society (page 143).
- Much has been written about organisations (pages 144–150).
- This will tell you that:
  - there isn't a single 'fits-all-situations' leadership style
  - the style that you use will be influenced by factors related to: the organisation's culture, history and size; the situation; the followers; the relationships that you have with them (page 152).
- Leading an organisation will be probably one of the most demanding tasks that you'll face in your working lifetime (page 153).
- There are a lot of teams in our organisations (page 155).
- These teams either:
  - control or run something, or
  - make something, or
  - do something, or
  - evaluate something and make recommendations about it (page 155).
- Teams are popular because they have the potential to enable you to:
  - tap into the skills, abilities and creativity of all the

people in them, and
- use all of those to greater effect in the workplace (page 157).

● As is so with their counterparts in organisations, team leaders:
- co-ordinate
- guide and advise
- create an 'umbrella' under which the team can operate
- fight to get adequate resources for the team
- coach, encourage and develop team members
- act as a problem-solving resource
- recognise and acknowledge good work
- provide an example of 'how things ought to be done' (page 159).

● In some teams, however, the leadership role becomes one that:
- is carried by different team members for different tasks or parts of a task
- is carried by different team members at different times in the teams' development (page 159).

Skills checkout

Doing, rather than just reading about, the things that you've examined in this chapter will be another demanding but worthwhile task. It will need you to continue to develop, refine and expand your individual 'bundle' of skills. If you think about what you've read you soon realise that these will include skills such as:

planning	thinking strategically
communicating	consulting
influencing and persuading	monitoring
problem solving	leading by example

obtaining/providing feedback	motivating
valuing and supporting	managing conflict
following	coaching
mentoring	empowering
learning	inspiring
involving others	setting objectives

All of these are needed for Units B5, B6, B7 and B9 of the Providing Direction section of the UK National Occupational Standards for Management and Leadership.

09

Who's following and why?

This chapter looks at the relationship between leaders and followers. It starts by taking a look at the nature of followership and then examines the influence of factors such as power, motivation, persuasion, influence, equality and diversity.

In the beginning

Let's start with a story – a young woman is waiting to be called into her interview for a job with a prestigious multinational corporation. She's anxious – her qualifications could be better and she has limited relevant experience. Her anxiety grows when she learns from other candidates that the interviewers will ask for examples of her leadership ability.

However, when the question is asked in the interview, an inspired reply leaps to her lips: 'I'm not a leader – but I am a terrific follower'.

She gets the job.

This is a story with at least two messages: firstly, it hints at the fact that, in the grand scheme of things, followers can be as important as leaders and, secondly, it tells us that it takes courage and initiative to be an effective follower.

It's in the nature of things that there are – and always will be – more followers than leaders. It's also worth noting that leaders have to have followers. But the why's and wherefore's of followership – or being a follower – have attracted little interest. When you put 'followership' into your web browser you'll get around one-tenth of the hits that you'll get when you put in 'leadership'. So why is it that the follower role has attracted so little attention and why is it that our views of following and followership are coloured by the view that leaders matter but followers don't?

History and worldwide events carry some of the blame for this. World and other wars call for strong heroic leaders at the head of authoritarian hierarchies rich in compliant followers. Similarly, the rise of the transnational corporation complete with its serried ranks of 'organisation men' (and women) led to the myth of lifelong job security in return for obedience and unquestioning loyalty.

But world events can also act in opposite ways.

Takeovers, recessions, bank crises and other events have led to none of our jobs being secure and to the flattening of traditional corporate pyramids. One result has been that power and responsibility have been delegated, often without prior training, down to people who, traditionally, had been 'leader dependent'. The results showed that new forms of leader/follower relationship – such as Transactional or Leader/Follower Exchange or Transformational leadership (see Chapter 2 – What's it all about?) – were needed. All of this has also led to an increasing recognition that the study of followership is as important as the study of leadership.

Followership

Let's start this section by getting a clearer idea of what following is about.

If you use your dictionary to do that you'll find statements that tell you that a follower is: *'one who follows another in regard to his teaching or opinions; an adherent or disciple; also one who follows an example, model, rule of conduct, etc.'*

However, as you'll soon see, there are various ways of doing this. Some 30 years ago in a seminal article – 'In Praise of Followers' – Robert Kelley suggested in the *Harvard Business Review* that the best followers display and use the skills of:

- self-management
- commitment
- competence building
- focusing their efforts towards maximum impact
- courage, honesty and credibility.

But Kelley also suggested that there were other sorts of followers – who were less effective (see Table 9.1 and Further Information and Reading).

Table 9.1: Followership patterns suggested by Robert Kelley

Passive followers or sheep – passive, uncritical, do what they are told to do and then stop.

Conformist followers or yes people – livelier than sheep but just as unenterprising, can be obsequiously deferential to leaders.

Alienated followers – critical, independent but 'turned-off' and passive.

Survivors – live by the motto 'better safe than sorry'.

Exemplary or effective followers – critical, independent and self-managing.

Other, later, views of how to categorise followers have included those of Barbara Kellerman (Table 9.2 and Further Information and Reading) who tells us that followers could be defined by both their rank – they hold jobs that are low in the organisational 'pecking' order – and the ways in which they behave.

It's some of these behaviours that we'll now look at.

Table 9.2: Barbara Kellerman's follower categories

Isolates – detached, not interested in leaders, know and do very little, survive by doing just enough to escape attention.

Bystanders – observe but don't participate, are aware of what's going on.

Participants – engaged in support or opposition.

Activists – bring energy and commitment either in support or opposition.

Diehards – prepared to 'go down with their cause', can be supporters or opponents.

Hard and soft

If you think about the sort of things that happen in your organisation you'll soon agree with Jon Katzenbach's suggestion (see Further Information and Reading) that these can be divided up into two broad groups.

First, there are the 'hard' or formal things – such as job descriptions, operating procedures, pay scales, organisation charts, performance measures, project management plans and techniques, cash flow and return on investment measures and process flow charts. Associated with these you'll find a cluster of disciplines or knowledge bases that are rich in 'hard' technology and terminology – such as finance, accounting, engineering, technology and operations management. Acting together, these make up the 'nuts and bolts' of the structure and operations of most organisations.

But second, and just as important, you'll find the 'soft' or informal things. These are all the things that you can't and don't make rules about – the human side of your organisation. They consist of the emotions, behaviours, joys and frustrations that come with working in an organisation; they include your organisation's myths, legends and fables and culture, and they embrace the uncharted and informal networks that enable you to say, 'Ah, but I know a man who does' and find out what's happening before it's formally announced. Together these are at least as powerful as the formal features of your organisation; sometimes – at times of change or crisis – they can be more significant. However, they don't have – in any formal sense – a cluster of associated disciplines or knowledge bases, unless you count our individual life experiences.

There's lots of evidence to indicate that organisational success comes when you keep these hard and soft sides in balance. If you are interested in creating that balance for the organisation or workgroup that you lead, a good place to start is by taking a look at some of the behaviours that go on there. Some of these – influencing, persuading, using power and motivating – are particularly significant when it comes to the relationship between you and your followers.

The influence spectrum

Influencing somebody is a common enough process and there are, as your experience will tell you, a number of ways in which you can do that. But, however you do it, there's a common objective for your actions. For when you exert influence, what you're trying to do is to generate change. This can be a change in the way people behave, the way they feel about things, what their opinions are or what they do. Think about how you influence the people around you and you'll soon realise that the ways that you use to do that fall into a spectrum of influence (see Figure 9.1).

- Education
- Persuasion
- Seduction
- Manipulation
- Propaganda
- Subversion
- Coercion

DONE WITH

DONE TO

Figure 9.1: The influence spectrum

This is a spectrum that has, at its extremes, two very different sorts of influence process:

- **Co-operative** processes – these are done **with** people – as in education or training.
- **Coercive** processes – these are done **to** people, as in forcing or compelling someone to do something.

It's easy enough to find examples of these in the workplace: disciplinary procedures are, for example, done *to* people, and training is done *with* people. Dig a little deeper and you'll find further differences between these examples. For discipline is punitive or punishing, aiming to stop people behaving in certain ways, while training is about individual growth and development aiming to encourage people to act in certain ways. When you think about this, you'll soon realise that the level of autonomy or the degree of individual freedom that you have to respond to influence changes as you move through this spectrum. You will have a high level of autonomy at the 'done-with' end and a low level at the 'done-to' end.

Influence shows up wherever you find people. But, as a leader, you're not going to get people to 'sign up' to your vision unless you accept and acknowledge their freedom to make their own choices. But even when you do that you may still have to use one of the more significant of the influence processes – persuasion.

Persuasion

Persuasion, at its core, is a form of influence and as such it's about creating change. Persuasion also happens quite a lot wherever you find people. It seems to be an integral part of the 'warp and weft' of all our lives.

However, persuasion also has a bad reputation. It's often seen as unethical, unsavoury, underhand or manipulative. It's usually associated with being seduced away from what you really want. You are persuaded – 'despite your better judgement' as is often said – to do or to accept something.

But the sort of persuasion that you're going to use as a leader isn't going to be like that. For here, in the twenty-first century, you work *with* – rather than command – your co-workers and you seek to empower them rather than dominate or manipulate them. All of this should tell you that using and developing the sort of persuasion that *isn't* manipulative is a key step on the road to becoming an effective leader in the workplace.

In Figure 9.1 you saw that persuasion is towards the 'done-with' end of the influence spectrum. This means that it has an implicit and high level of individual independence or autonomy. As a result, when you use this sort of persuasion you will need to accept that people are free to decide things for themselves. Once you accept this, a whole raft of actions that are based on domination, bullying, and coercion of any kind, propaganda and, even that grand old standby of our interpersonal relationships, manipulation, all become unacceptable. But that's not all. For if you really think this through you'll find that it means that, when you accept the autonomy of an individual, you – as a leader – can no longer fall back upon the authority of your role to ensure compliance or gain acceptance.

For many of you this will be a big step to take. Nevertheless, it's a 'must do' one. For this sort of persuasion is *not* done *to* someone else but undertaken *with* them. It's a complex two-way process in which the role boundaries of all involved become blurred and viewpoints change. It's also a process that, as you'll now see, has the following fundamental principles – principles that tell you that, as a leader, you need to:

- recognise that persuasion is an act of communication – and that, as you saw earlier in this book (see Chapter 7 – Can you hear me?), means that it is a shared two-way process
- accept that persuasion is a conscious act that respects the autonomy of everyone involved
- acknowledge that the desired outcome of persuasion is change
- be conscious of the fact that the roles of persuader and persuadee are interchangeable.

Remember these and you'll find that your persuasions will be done *with* someone – rather than *to* them. It's also worth making sure that your persuasion:

- is clearly expressed and well organised
- uses examples – the sort of 'done-before' examples that reach people
- stresses the positives – but doesn't lie about or hide the negatives
- promises rewards – they generate positive results while penalties lead to negativity and nothing leads to nothing.

It's also worth remembering that research tells us that we are most easily persuaded by people who:

- we like or respect
- have power over us
- are willing to do 'tit for tat' deals with us.

Use Figure 9.2 (page 172) to check out your persuasion.

Power

We've all got power – in one form or another. We can, as you'll soon see, have this power for any one of a number of reasons. But, whatever its form or nature, the essence of this power lies in its ability to produce effects. The power that happens in organisations is usually called 'social' power. It's a basic and common element of all our social relationships and arises out of our connections to each other. It can, of course, be either negative or positive – the power to destroy or the power to create – and in any one situation the 'balance of power' can be such that you can have more or less power than someone else.

Social power acts in one of two different ways. When we have power it brings with it the ability to:

- influence others in ways that further our own interests, or
- resist the activities of others.

Self Evaluation Questionnaire

Circle the number that is nearest to the way that you feel about each aspect of persuasion.

Preparation

I'm clear about the outcome that I want to achieve	1 2 3 4 5 6 7	I'm not sure why I'm doing this
I'm clear about who I want to persuade	1 2 3 4 5 6 7	I'm not sure who I ought to talk to
I've found out about their background	1 2 3 4 5 6 7	I've no idea what their background is

Doing it

I'm prepared to modify my desired outcome	1 2 3 4 5 6 7	I will persuade them to do what I want
I'll listen to what they say	1 2 3 4 5 6 7	I expect them to listen to me
This is something that we are doing together	1 2 3 4 5 6 7	I'm doing it to them

Scoring

If your total score comes to 18 or less then you appear to be persuading well. Scores of 24 and above indicate that you are having some problems.

Figure 9.2: Persuasion

Here are some examples of social power:

- **Position or legitimate power** – you get this when you're appointed to a role or position in your organisation but you only have it for as long as you stay in that role or position. The amount of this power depends upon:
  - the authority given to that role by the organisation, and
  - the power of the organisation.
- **Resource power** – you have this sort of power if you possess or control something that's needed or valued by someone, somewhere – a resource.
- **Expert power** – you get this sort of power when you acquire or develop special knowledge or skills that are needed by others.
- **Personal or charismatic power** – this is the power that you possess by virtue of being the person you are – see Charisma Theory in Table 2.1.
- **Reward power** – this comes from your ability to grant rewards – for favours or services rendered, hardships endured or an above-average performance. Usually comes hand–in–hand with position and resource power.
- **Connection power** – this is about 'who-you-know' and is found in relationships, networking and politics and often related to or associated with position, personal or expert power.
- **Coercive power** – involves the use of force or threats to control what people do and is a crude but, nevertheless, often used form of power. Despite its common usage, coercive power has little real value for a leader.

All power brings with it the potential for abuse. As someone once said, 'Power tends to corrupt, and absolute power corrupts absolutely' and there are plenty of examples – such the former US President Richard Nixon – of the misuse of power.

You can see from all of this that both leaders and followers are significant players in the 'power game'. In addition to all of the above sources of power, leaders can have a 'this is my vision' sort of power and followers can have the 'No, we don't agree' sort of power. However, it's worth remembering that leaders cannot be powerful without the consent and support of their followers. Put simply, you, as a leader, will only have power if your followers give it to you.

Motivation

Motivation is another of those things that's woven into the warp and weft of all our lives. As a result, a lot has been written and said about motivation, leading to a considerable number of theories about what does – and doesn't – motivate people. Not surprisingly, most of these have been aimed at providing answers to questions like 'Why do people come to work?' and 'How can we get them to work better?'

One of the more accessible of these theories is that of Abraham Maslow. At the core of his view is the idea that the key to motivating you lies in answering your needs. We all have needs. They generate our goals, our end points, our winning lines. Maslow divided these needs into five groups:

- physiological needs
- safety needs
- love needs
- esteem needs, and finally
- self-actualisation needs.

These, he said, act upon you in the order that they're given above. That is you are motivated to act in ways that satisfy your physiological needs – for warmth, food and water – before you begin to seek answers to your 'higher' needs such as job security, prestige and the freedom to create. It's almost as if these needs are 'stacked', one above another, as in a pyramid (see Figure 9.3). You act in ways that aim to get your needs answered in their order on the 'pyramid' and, once answered, they lose – at least for the time being – their potency. But, as someone, somewhere once said, life's never quite that simple. For if you think about it you'll probably realise that you know or have heard or read about people for whom:

- self-esteem is more important than love, or
- the freedom to create is more important then being 'safe', or
- high ideals or beliefs are more important than having enough food or being safe or well regarded.

What these apparent contradictions tell you is something that you probably know already – that people are complicated. It also tells you that you need to take a look at some of the other ideas about the how and why of people's motivation.

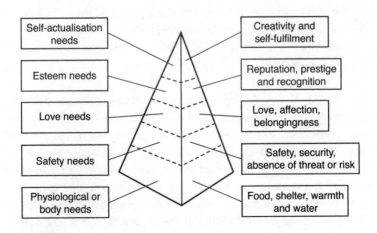

Figure 9.3: Maslow's pyramid of needs

Theory X and Theory Y

Douglas McGregor suggested that the way you are managed is based upon a number of assumptions that your manager makes about your needs or goals. He put these assumptions into two groups: Theory X and Theory Y.

Theory X managers believe that you:

- don't like work and will avoid it if you can
- need to be coerced, controlled, directed in order to get you to put in a reasonable amount of effort at work
- prefer to be told what to do
- have little ambition, and
- want, above all, to be secure.

Theory Y managers are quite different. They assume that:

- working is natural, as natural as, say, playing or resting
- you have the capacity to be self-directing and self-controlling
- you can learn to seek and enjoy responsibility
- the ability to be creative isn't limited to a precious few
- most jobs and work situations only use part of your potential.

It's obvious that these sets of assumptions are radically different. Theory X and its traditional 'control' style of management has also been described as the 'carrot and stick' theory – a carrot to tempt and a stick to beat. Theory Y with its delegating style of management has been likened to the more modern empowerment style of management. The style or theory that you – as a leader – are inclined to choose will depend upon your own experience of being managed and the culture of the organisation that you work in (see Chapter 10 – How do you do it?). Be warned though, for using the Theory X style will not result in you being an effective leader.

Hygiene and motivation

Fredrick Herzberg's views about what does – and doesn't – motivate people at work are said to have come out of the stories that people told him about what made them feel satisfied or dissatisfied there. When he analysed these stories he found that:

- Good times were associated with:
  - achievement
  - advancement
  - recognition
  - responsibility, and
  - work itself.
- Bad times were associated with:
  - poor company policy
  - low salaries
  - lack of security
  - poor working conditions, and
  - poor work relationships.

You've already seen some of these in Maslow's groups of needs and in McGregor's Theories X and Y. Herzberg then concluded that people are driven by two basic but quite different needs:

- the need to avoid pain, and
- the need to self-actualise.

The first of these – the need to avoid pain – relates to what are called 'hygiene' or 'maintenance' factors. These include:

- what your working conditions are like
- how much you get paid
- how you are supervised, and
- how you get on with your co-workers.

According to Herzberg, these factors only have the potential to motivate you negatively. What this tells you, as a leader, is that they will de-motivate your followers if they aren't there or aren't of adequate quality. However, when you increase a hygiene factor the effect that you'll get will be temporary and short-term. Doing this will be like taking a headache tablet – a temporary relief – though in this case the headache is meaningless work.

The second need – the need to self-actualise – relates to factors that are called 'motivators'. These act positively, they create satisfaction and they encourage you to work better. Motivators include:

- the sense of achievement you get when you've done a good job
- the recognition you get from those around you in the workplace
- the meaningfulness, variety or significance of the work you do
- the responsibility you are given – or take – for doing that work, and
- your chances of being promoted because of the work you've done.

You've probably spotted that these factors correspond, by and large, to the upper part of Maslow's staircase of needs – the needs concerned with esteem and self-actualisation. If you've got these in your relationship with your followers then they'll probably feel needed and encouraged.

Expectations and hopes

People, as you've already seen, are complicated. They have and display a considerable variety of temperaments, styles, preferences, needs and expectations. For some people, money is the major incentive while for others *the* major incentive lies in striving to achieve the impossible and, in so doing, extending their experience and abilities. Whatever the individual goals of your followers are, you, as a leader, need to be aware that they'll exert a considerable influence on their behaviour. They'll behave in the ways that they do because of:

- the goals they've selected for themselves, and
- what they've learned about achieving these goals.

Edward Lawler's view is that your followers' motivation to perform well at work is determined by:

- how probable they think it is that a given amount of effort will result in them getting a reward, and
- whether they will or won't want the reward that's on offer.

In another set of ideas Victor Vroom tells you that the way your followers behave is affected by:

- what they want to happen
- their guesses about how likely certain events – including the outcome that they want – are to happen, and
- how strongly they believe that the outcome they want will satisfy their needs.

However, one of the problems with these and sets of ideas like them is that they assume that we all think logically and behave rationally. Life, and your own experience, will have told you that isn't always so.

So where do all these ideas about motivation get you when it comes to motivating your followers?

The answer starts to emerge when you recognise that these followers are individuals; individuals with:

- different ways of doing things

- different values, and
- different sets of hopes and desires.

However, the key question here is not 'How different are these followers?' but 'How can each of them be helped to improve their performance?' You'll notice that *help* is used here, rather than *managed* or *directed* or *controlled*. If you doubt the wisdom of this then take at look at the sort of things that your followers do when they are not at work. You'll probably find the range of these is impressive. They'll do things like sing in a choir, run a troop of scouts, study for a qualification, build model planes, learn to play the piano and breed stick insects. They'll do these because they want to – rather than to earn money – and they do them in ways that are self-managed, creative and energetic – rather than 'by the book'. The next step is for you to recognise that your followers:

- don't just come to work for the money
- do want to achieve
- need to work towards targets that are meaningful to them
- have the potential to do more than they have been allowed to do so far, and
- are capable of accepting more responsibility than they've been given so far.

You also need to recognise that they work better when they:

- direct, and
- control their own work.

Equality and diversity

The stresses and strains of the marketplace of the early twenty-first century have made organisational survival and growth a challenging task. At the same time it has become evident that success will only be achieved if the people who make up our organisations are encouraged and allowed to use their creativity and resourcefulness to the full. Yet the population from which these people are drawn has changed – it's become more ethnically diverse and the average age has risen. New patterns of migration have changed what were previously culturally and ethnically homogeneous communities. One result of this has been that discrimination and prejudice have raised their ugly heads. As a result, equality legislation has been introduced and has helped to challenge much of this.

Nevertheless, the issues of equality of opportunity and diversity (see Table 9.3) remain as key factors in the relationship between any leader and his/her followers.

Table 9.3: Equality of opportunity and diversity

Equality of opportunity comes about when individuals or groups of individuals are treated in ways that are fair, equal and no less favourable with specific reference to their needs, including areas of race, gender, disability, religion or belief, sexual orientation and age.

Diversity recognition should accept, respect and value individual differences to contribute and encourage the realisation of their full potential by promoting an inclusive culture.

The benefits of getting these concepts integrated into the culture of your organisation are considerable. Doing this won't just enable you to be seen as complying with equality legislation, it will also:

- kick-start the release of the full potential of your followers
- enable you to be seen by all as a fair, forward looking and ethical leader.

To achieve this integration you, as a leader, are going to have to:

- make a clear and overt policy statement about equality of opportunity and diversity
- make sure that this is implemented in your area of responsibility or organisation.

Doing this won't be easy. It may, for example, mean that you'll need to change your ideas about what is and what isn't prejudice. It will also mean that you'll need to set an example by your own behaviour, words and actions; an example that places a positive value on diversity in both the workforce and the community at large. But it will be worthwhile. After all, as someone said, these people don't just work for the organisation – they *are* that organisation.

Chapter checklist

In this chapter you've taken a look at the relationship between leading and following and the factors that influence that relationship. Use the list below to check where you've got to. If you've missed something or don't understand it go back to the page given and read through it again.

- The relationship between a leader and followers is an important though neglected one (page 162).
- There are a number of views about both the nature and the types of followers (pages 165–166).
- Organisational success comes when you keep the hard or formal and the soft or informal sides of the organisation in balance (page 166).
- One way of creating that balance is to pay attention to the behaviours that go on there (page 167).
- The extreme ends of the influence spectrum are:

- **co-operative** processes – these are done *with* people, as in education or training
- **coercive** processes – these are done *to* people, as in forcing or compelling someone to do something (page 168).
- Persuasion is a form of influence (page 169).
- You, as a leader, need to:
  - recognise that persuasion is an act of communication and that, as you saw earlier in this book, means it is a shared two-way process
  - accept that persuasion is a conscious act that respects the autonomy of everyone involved
  - acknowledge that the desired outcome of persuasion is a change
  - be conscious of the fact that the roles of persuader and persuadee are interchangeable (page 170).
- The sort of power that happens in organisations is usually called 'social' power (page 171).
- Power can come from your:
  - postion or role
  - access to resources
  - expertise
  - personality
  - access to rewards
  - connections
  - use of force or threats (page 173).
- What does or doesn't motivate people has been described by:
  - Maslow (page 174)
  - McGregor (page 176)
  - Herzberg (page 177)
  - Lawler (page 179), and
  - Vroom (page 179).
- Equality of opportunity and diversity are key factors in the relationship between any leader and his/her followers (page 180).

Skills checkout

The relationship between a leader and his or her followers is as complex and demanding as most relationships are. As such it will need you to continue to develop, refine and expand your individual 'bundle' of skills. If you think about what you've read you soon realise that these will include skills such as:

planning	thinking strategically
risk management	communicating
consulting	influencing and persuading
monitoring	evaluating
problem solving	leading by example
obtaining/providing feedback	motivating
valuing and supporting	managing conflict
following	balancing competing needs
mentoring	empowering
learning	inspiring
involving others	building consensus
decision making	information management
prioritising	reviewing and reporting

Most of these are needed for Units B9, B11 and B12 of the Providing Direction section of the UK National Occupational Standards for Management and Leadership.

How do you do it?

Style, or how you do what you do, is one of the many ways that you express your individuality. As such, it can exert a considerable influence over both the nature and the effectiveness of your workplace leading. This chapter looks at several of the ways in which style can be described and explores the influence that it exerts upon your workplace leading.

What's it all about?

Style is one of those words that appears in many guises. But when it comes to leadership the one that matters is the one that tells you that it's *'a manner of executing a task or performing an action or operation'*.

This tells you that your leadership style is the way that you do that leading or, to put it another way, the way you do what you do when you lead others. Research tells us that leadership style is a collection or accumulation of 'micro-behaviours' and that, as such, it's a relatively stable and long-lasting pattern of behaviour. You can, of course, choose what style you want to use when you're leading. But, for that style to be successful, it will need to be based upon:

- your personal preferences, and
- factors such as where and with whom you're doing it and what role you're carrying out when you do it.

Nevertheless, we are all creatures of habit and it has been observed that some elements of your individual style tend to persist and stay with you, wherever you are and whatever you are doing.

My way

The style that you choose to adopt for your leading is a significant factor when it comes to its effectiveness. So, before we move on to look at the ways in which these styles are described, it's worth taking a moment to look back at what you've already read about style and leadership.

You've already read (Chapter 2 – What's it all about?) about three basic styles of leadership:

- authoritarian, autocratic or directive style
- participative or democratic style
- delegating, empowering or 'laissez-faire' style.

You've also, in Chapter 9 – Who's following and why? – read about Theory X and Theory Y managers who adopt styles that are based on assumptions about whether you don't or do like work. You've also discovered that your choice of leadership style will be influenced by a variety of things such as:

- how much time is available
- whether workgroup relationships are good
- who's got the information – you, your fellow workers, or both

- whether your fellow workers are self-starters and have the ability to analyse the situation and determine what needs to be done and how to do it
- what sort of task you're facing – is it structured or unstructured, complicated or simple, new or done before?

One of the ways that the available range of leadership styles can be illustrated is shown in Figure 10.1.

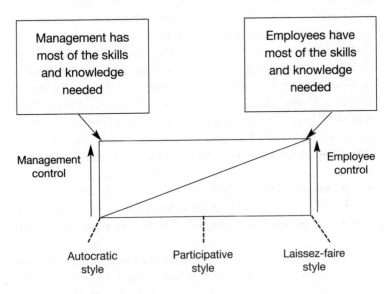

Figure 10.1: Leadership styles

But these aren't the only factors that are relevant to or influence your choice of leadership style. Your personality and your experience are just as significant when it comes to the choice that you make about the style that you use to lead.

Psychologically speaking

Our individual personalities can be described as dynamic sets of characteristics that significantly influence the way we see and react to the world around us. There are, of course, lots of theories about personalities.

Carl Jung – the founder of analytical psychology – developed one of the more accessible of these theories in the 1920s. Jung popularised the concepts of extraverts – who, for example, tend to enjoy human interactions and to be enthusiastic, talkative and gregarious – and introverts – who tend to be solitary, low-key, deliberate and less engaged in social situations. These ideas have persisted and now appear in virtually all of the ways used to describe personality, such as Cattell's 16 Personality Factors, the Minnesota Multiphasic Personality Inventory and the Myers–Briggs Type Indicator. Jung also suggested that people could be categorised in terms of four main functions of consciousness; two of which (Sensation (S) and Intuition(I)) he described as perceiving functions while the other two (Thinking (T) and Feeling (F)) he described as judging functions. These functions are modified by the attitudes of extraversion – which is also called extroversion – and introversion. In their most basic form, they enable us to identify four 'people-pictures':

- **ST individuals** – combine sensation and thought and are often described as logical, arriving at conclusions on the basis of 'hard' facts.
- **IT individuals** – combine thought and intuition and shape their conclusions with ideas and insights, rather than facts, and are concerned with the possibilities of a situation.
- **IF individuals** – have views of the world that are strongly influenced by intuition and feelings and are more concerned with values than facts.
- **SF individuals** – combine sensing and feelings, concerned with the evidence of their senses and use their 'gut' feelings.

The American psychologists, Katharine Briggs and Isabel Briggs Myers modified and extended these basic 'people-pictures' in the 1940s to create a personality test that claims to tell you how a person prefers to work. When you take this test – the Myers-Briggs Type Indicator or MBTI – the results are said to identify which of 16 possible psychological types you appear to fit into. These are based on the following pairs of preferences:

Extraversion (E) ——— Introversion (I)
Sensing (S) ——— Intuition (N)
Thinking (T) ——— Feeling (F)
Judging (J) ——— Perceiving (P)

Other writers have annexed these into five basic managerial styles whose outlines and associated Myers–Briggs acronyms are shown in Table 10.1.

Table 10.1: The five basic managerial styles

Traditionalist (ISTJ, ISFJ, ESTJ, ESFJ) – practical managers who weigh up risks and consequences before taking a decision and are keen on order. Very good at handling data and co-ordinating but not good with change.

Troubleshooter (ISTP, ESTP) and **Negotiator** (ISFP, ESFP) – both problem solvers who are very flexible and able to live in the 'here and now' but can appear unpredictable and disorganised.

Catalyst (INFJ, INFP, ENFP, ENFJ) – the communicators of the workplace who care for people but may base their decisions on values rather than facts.

Visionary (INTJ, INTP, ENTP, ENTJ) – the planners, innovators and creators of the workplace, good decision takers but may need to be reminded about other people's problems.

However, these have been criticised as being vague and general and oversimplifying what is an extremely complex and dynamic picture. Other workers, such as David Keirsey, focused more on behaviour than feelings and expanded on the MBTI descriptions. For example, Keirsey's descriptions of his four temperaments (Artisans, Guardians, Idealists and Rationals), which he correlated with the 16 MBTI personality types, are said to show how these temperaments differ in terms of language use, intellectual orientation, educational and vocational interests, social orientation, self-image, personal values, social roles, and even characteristic hand gestures.

Another view of personality comes from the work of Carl Rogers (see Further Information and Reading). Rogers (with Abraham Maslow) was widely credited as being one of the founders of the humanistic approach to psychology and developed what became known as the 'person-centred' approach to understanding personality and relationships. This approach aims to enable a growth-promoting climate with open communication, valuing of diversity and creativity and the empowerment of people in order to achieve their highest potential. It's an approach that's been applied in individual, organisational and group settings across a wide range of fields including social change, cross-cultural communications, personal growth, education, counselling and psychotherapy.

When it comes to leadership, Rogers and his followers argue that this approach has the potential to both release and facilitate open communication and valuing diversity. These skills are said to enable leadership that's:

- **authentic** and makes possible a climate of 'realness' and 'transparency' as well as fostering trust and commitment
- **non-judgemental** and gives rise to a nurturing climate of acceptance, fostering creativity, diversity, new thinking and productive processes
- **empathic** with a deep understanding that enables a

climate of open communication, fostering value, recognition and worth.

The psychiatrist Alfred Adler also wrote about our individual 'styles of life'. These, he said, reflect individual, unique, unconscious and repetitive ways of responding to (or avoiding) the main tasks of living: friendship, love, and work. Our style, he said, is what we are, who we are, what we want to be. He identified four primary styles:

- **ruling** type – aggressive, dominating people who manipulate situations and people to get their way
- **getting** type – people who take selfishly without giving back
- **avoiding** type – people who hate being defeated, may be successful, but have not taken any risks getting there
- **socially useful** type – people with a great deal of social interest and activity.

Adler described the first three of these styles as 'mistaken styles'.

By now, you'll be a good way down the road towards a clearer idea of just how important the influence of style is for your workplace leading. If you're still uncertain about this, reflect for a moment upon what the differences were between the good and bad leaders that you've experienced. Some of them would have treated you with respect, listening to whatever you said and then responding. Others would have treated you like a robot. You'll probably remember that it wasn't so much what they did that counted but the way that they did it. In other words, it was their style that mattered.

So let's move on now to look, in more detail, at some of the views about the influence of your leadership style. These will include:

- Managerial Grid
- Transactional analysis

- Role theory
- Assertiveness
- Ethical leading.

Managerial Grid

The Managerial Grid (see Figure 10.2) is another way of looking at the options that you have for your leadership style. This was developed in the 1960s, by Robert Blake and Jane Mouton (see Further Information and Reading), as a self-completion questionnaire-based diagnostic tool that allows managers to assess, review and possibly change their leadership style. It suggests that there are five different basic leadership styles, each of which is identified in relation to the dimensions of 'concern for people' and 'concern for production'.

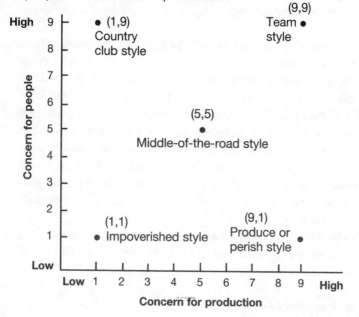

Figure 10.2: The Managerial Grid

The different styles shown in this figure are:

- **Dictatorial or produce or perish style (9,1)** – a manager with this style will use the skills of planning, scheduling and organising to keep the human factors to a minimum.
- **Sound or team management style (9,9)** – this style attempts to balance human and task needs.
- **Accommodating or country club style (1,9)** – this style has a high concern for people and a low concern for production. Managers using this style pay a lot of attention to the security and comfort of the employees in hopes that this will increase performance.
- **Indifferent or impoverished style (1,1)** – managers who use this style have low concern for both people and production. Often used to avoid getting into trouble or to try and stay in the same job for a long time.
- **Status quo or middle-of-the-road style (5,5)** – this style tries to balance the goals of the organisation and the needs and wants of the workers.

Two further styles have also been identified:

- **Opportunistic style** – this is based on exploitation and manipulation and doesn't have a fixed location on the grid. People who use it are said to adopt whatever behaviour offers the greatest personal benefit.
- **Paternalistic style** – this, the 'prescribe and guide' style, was a later addition to the grid and is said to alternate between the (1,9) and (9,1) locations. People who use this style praise and support but discourage challenges to their thinking.

Blake and Mouton suggested that the sound or team management style (9,9) is the best way to manage. In its fullest form, this style moves beyond simply supervising staff and setting tasks into using the full range of leadership skills.

I'm OK – You're OK

Transactional analysis (TA) was created and developed by the American psychiatrist Eric Berne (see Further Information and Reading) during the late 1950s. It uses the 'ego-state' model or Parent–Adult–Child model to describe the way that you and I are structured psychologically and employs this model to make suggestions about the how and why of our relationships.

TA says that we all have three ego-states. These are:

- **Parent** – an ego state in which we will behave, feel and think in response to our memories of how our parents acted.
- **Adult** – in this 'ideal' ego state we draw on all of the resources and experiences of our lives as adults. It's the ideal ego state that responds and reacts to what's happening in the 'here-and-now' rather than a remembered past or a 'might be' future. This is the ego state that TA aims to strengthen.
- **Child** – an ego state in which we behave, feel and think in ways that are similar to our childhood patterns.

These ego states are, of course, not actual adults, parents, or children and are denoted by using capital letters – as in Parent (P), Adult (A) and Child (C). Within each ego state there are subdivisions – as in a nurturing Parent – who gives permission and security, or a critical Parent who makes negative comparisons to family traditions or ideals. These subdivisions are useful when it comes to describing behaviour patterns, feelings, and ways of thinking. They can be positive and beneficial (functional) or counterproductive and negative (dysfunctional).

TA also uses the ideas of 'transactions' and 'strokes' to describe some of the ways by which we interact with each other. Transactions are the flow patterns of these interactions while strokes are the recognition, attention or responses that you and the person you're interacting with give to each other. Transactions can take place at both the overt (open) level and the hidden (psychological) level and the strokes involved can be positive or negative. Depending on the sort of strokes within them, the transactions of your interaction with another person can be experienced as being either positive or negative. These transactions are important – even to the point where a negative transaction is felt to be better than no transaction – and can be portrayed as in Figure 10.3 .

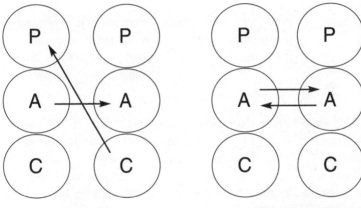

Crossed
transaction

Complementary
transaction

Figure 10.3: Transactions

When you look at this figure you'll see that the communication flow lines are parallel and reciprocal in a complementary transaction. In a crossed transaction, however, the communications are crossed and are aimed at the ego state that the addressee thinks the other is in, rather than the ego state that they actually are in. Crossed transactions cause problems. Table 10.2 also summarises some of the things that get said and done in these transactions by each of the ego states.

Table 10.2: Ego state characteristics

Ego state	Words used	Gestures used
Parent	Always, never, should, shouldn't, don't, right, wrong	Pointing finger, arms folded across chest, sighing, patting another on head
Adult	Could, possible, true, probable, test, I think	Listening, continual movement of face, eyes and body
Child	Want, let's, wish, guess, dream, funny, magic, great, super	Whining voice, downcast eyes, teasing laughter, shrugging shoulders, asks for permission to speak

TA also suggests that each of us has a 'Script' and a 'Life Position'. A script is described as the life plan that you chose for yourself in childhood. It has a particular end-point or 'pay-off'. Your script was often reinforced or confirmed by your parents and your childhood experiences. In adult life, however, you will rarely be aware of its influence or contents. Nevertheless, it will influence how you see and communicate with the world around you. The same could be said of your life position. This draws strongly on your script and tells you about yourself and your relationship to others. There are said to be four basic life positions as follows:

1. I'm not OK – You're OK
2. I'm not OK – You're not OK
3. I'm OK – You're not OK
4. I'm OK – You're OK

TA suggests that, for most people, the 'I'm not OK – You're OK' life position – that's common in childhood – is the one that persists into their adult life.

TA also tells us about the 'games' that we often play with each other. These are described as sequences of complementary transactions that proceed towards a predictable outcome. Berne identified dozens of games, each of which had a 'pay-off' for those playing. These pay-offs could, for example, be about earning sympathy or satisfaction or vindication or some other emotion.

TA aims to provide an opportunity for you to change your life script and shift into the 'I'm OK – You're OK' position. In doing that TA takes up a goal-oriented position, rather than being a problem solving process. It aims to free you from your childhood script and to encourage spontaneity, intimacy, active problem-solving. It also provides an analytical framework from which you can view and review your leadership.

Role theory

Role theory tells us that everything we do in life involves us in acting out one or another of a set of socially defined roles. These roles bring with them a set of duties, expectations, norms and behaviours, all of which we are obliged to fulfil or enact when we carry out a role. The list of actual, possible and potential roles that we all face is almost endless. You, for example, could be a brother or a sister, a mother or a father, an accountant, salesperson, social worker, engineer or, of course, a leader. When you carry out any one of these roles you'll find that the people around you will expect you to behave in certain ways. This set of behaviours will be relevant to the role you've taken on or been given. For example, if you are an accountant you'll be expected to do the things that accountants do – which, in the broadest sense, means that you'll measure and report on financial information. Similarly, if you are a leader you'll be expected to do all the things that this book has told you that you need to do. These expectations can act in ways that help you – as when people will see you as being an 'expert' on a particular subject because you've given a presentation about it, or hinder you – as when people don't expect you to express your feelings because that wouldn't be 'right' for the role you are carrying out.

But carrying out or doing these behaviours isn't all that's expected of you. The style that you adopt when you carry out a role is just as significant and important as what you do. You wouldn't, for example, expect your doctor to laugh when you told him about your ailment – you'd expect him or her to react seriously and with interest. So, the style of your doing – or the way that you do what you do – is important when it comes to roles.

Each of the roles that you carry out has a 'role set' associated with it. This, in its simplest form, consists of a group of associated roles that are carried out by other people. Figure 10.4 shows a simple example of a role set for the role of 'manager'. When you look at this role set what you'll see is that the roles in it cover a wide range of activities and will have an equally wide range of expectations. For example, the expectations that a trade union official will have of the role of a manager will be different from the expectations that a customer has of that role.

When you look at roles in a detached way you'll soon see that carrying out a role – any role – is a complicated business. On the one hand, there's a set of remarkably detailed, complex and often unwritten expectations for the role, while on the other hand, there's a considerable body of pressure for you to meet those expectations. The expectations that people have of leaders are, in principle, no different from the expectations that they have of the other roles that they meet in their lives or workplaces. If these expectations aren't met, complications – including disappointment – will follow. Nevertheless, despite all the complications and difficulties, we all manage to 'muddle through' and somehow meet the myriad expectations that are projected at us. As a result, roles – including that of the leader – are significant in our lives, both in and out of the workplace.

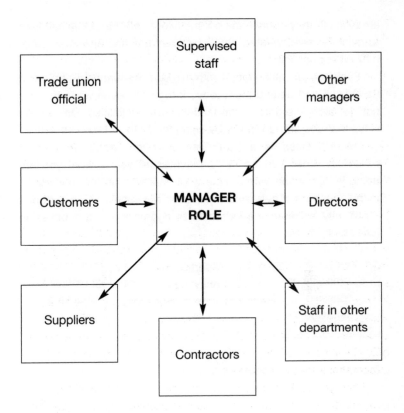

Figure 10.4: A role set

The middle way

The way things are these days, conflict is getting to be an all-too-common factor in the workplace. It will appear for any one of a number of reasons. For example, people may argue because one of them feels that the other keeps on shooting down their ideas; a manager may keep on making what appear to be sarcastic remarks; you may have a customer who persists in thwarting your attempts to help him. All of these and many other similar situations are difficult; they contain the potential for conflict and this can lead to disagreement, wasted time, poor performance and strained or difficult relationships.

Every leader will be faced with this sort of situation. People can be difficult and getting them to work together, even when they do not get along, is part of the leader's responsibilities. One of the ways that you can do this is by using the skills of being assertive.

Assertiveness is a particular behaviour style or way of behaving. When you do it – behave assertively – what you are doing is interacting with people while standing up for your rights. In the spectrum of behaviours assertion will appear at the midpoint – half-way between the extremes of aggression and submission (see Figure 10.5).

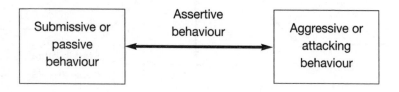

Figure 10.5: A spectrum of behaviours

These two extremes – submissiveness and aggression – are quite different:

- **Submissive behaviour** generally appears when people want to avoid or put off conflict. At its core it's about gaining the approval of others, avoiding hurting or upsetting anyone or 'de-fusing' an oncoming conflict. Words and phrases like, 'I'm sorry to take up your time but...' or 'Would you be upset if we...' get used and often have the effect of triggering aggression.
- **Aggressive behaviour** involves, in its more extreme forms, the use of sarcasm, adopting a patronising

attitude or dumping the blame for problems and mistakes on someone else. It can even take the form of physical aggression. Words and phrases like, 'Don't ask questions – just do it...', 'That's stupid' or 'Its nothing to do with me – it's all your fault' are common in aggressive behaviour.

Assertive behaviour, however, is quite different to these extremes:

- **Assertive behaviour** is exhibited by people who respect other people's right to express their ideas, feelings and needs, while also recognising that they too have the right to express their own ideas, feelings and needs.

So, being an assertive leader means:

- being honest with yourself and others, and
- having the ability to say directly what you want, need or feel – *but not at the expense of others*.

As an assertive leader you're going to have to learn to use the skill of negotiating in order to reach workable compromises with others. Doing this means having confidence in yourself and being positive while, at the same time, understanding other people's points of view. Assertive people use words and phrases like: 'I believe that... what do you think?', 'I would like to...' and 'What can we do to resolve this problem?' They also use body language in different ways (see Table 10.3).

Being assertive is actually a powerful social skill, a real expression of your individual style as a leader. But it's also a skill that:

- is situation specific – its use depends upon the nature of both the situation and the interaction
- involves both verbal and non-verbal communication
- involves taking risks – it may not produce the desired result.

Table 10.3: The behaviour spectrum

	Assertive	Aggressive	Passive
Posture	Upright, straight back	Leaning forward	Drawing away
Head	Firm but not rigid	Jutting chin	Head dropped down
Eyes	Direct with good and regular eye contact	Staring, often piercing or glaring	Little eye contact, lots of glancing away
Face	Expression fits with the words spoken	Set/firm	Smiling – even when upset
Voice	Well modulated to fit context	Loud or overloud and emphatic	Soft and hesitant, words trailing off at the end of sentence
Arms/hands	Relaxed/moving easily	Arm waving, finger pointing and jabbing	Still or aimless
Movement/ walking	Measured pace suitable to action	Slow and heavy or fast, deliberate, hard	Slow and hesitant or fast and jerky

Ethical leading

Look ethics up in the dictionary and you'll probably find a definition that tells you that these are *'the moral principles by which a person is guided'*. As such, ethics appears to be about the 'big ideas' such as good, bad, noble, ignoble, right, wrong, justice and virtue.

But these aren't the only things that ethics are about. As a leader you'll need to develop and demonstrate your own individual set of 'micro' ethics. These will be individual to you and they'll need to be specific and demonstrable – rather than broad brush or generalised. In short, they'll need to be an integral part of the way that you do your leading – your style. They'll also need to be allied to the ethics of your organisation or its corporate social responsibility (CSR) policy.

You've already seen (see Chapter 9 – Who's following and why?) how important it is to get issues like equality of opportunity and diversity integrated into the culture of your organisation. But the fine grain of your individual ethics should take this further. As a leader you can encourage and support a whole range of behaviours that demonstrate the need for and value of ethics. These could include car-sharing clubs for commuting employees, waste reduction by printing double-sided, turning off lights in empty rooms and turning the heating down, all of which will save money and help reduce a company's carbon footprint. The lean approach to reducing waste can be adopted — waste in space, cost, material, motion, process and inventory. Surveys tell us that being ethical also has other benefits, such as the fact that some clients and customers will find it appealing and that you may find it easier to recruit and retain staff.

Issues like ethics have, for a long time, been seen as irrelevant to the realities of corporate life. But the tide has now turned and for many employees an ethical workplace is a serious concern. As a result, leaders and organisations that ignore their ethical responsibilities do so at their peril.

At the end

You saw at the beginning of this chapter that the style you adopt in your leading is an individual and personal choice. It's a set of interwoven micro-behaviours that you alone have chosen to develop and adopt. You've done this for good reason – because you think or feel that this particular style results in what you see as effective leadership. Being effective here means that it gets the results that you desire. As a result, there are no classifications of 'right' or 'wrong' when it comes to your individual leading style. It will either do or won't do what you want it to and, in the end, that is what you must judge it by.

At this point, it might be worth revisiting Figure 1.1 and checking out that what you wrote there still stands.

Chapter checklist

In this chapter you've taken a look at style and some of the views about the ways, means and outcomes of its influence on the way that you lead.

Use the list below to check where you've got to. If you've missed something or don't understand it go back to the page given and read through it again.

- Style is about the way that you do what you do and is an individual collection of micro-behaviours (page 185).
- Your style, if it's going to be successful, will be based upon:
  - your personal preference, and
  - factors such as where and with whom you're doing it and what role you're carrying out when you do it (page 186)
- Your personality and your experience are significant when it comes to the choice that you make about the style that you use to lead (page 187).
- Ways of describing your personality and the ways it interacts with the world around it include those of:
  - Carl Jung
  - Katherine Briggs and Isabel Briggs Myers
  - David Keirsey
  - Carl Rogers

- Alfred Adler (pages 189–191).
- Views about the ways in which the influence of your leadership style get exerted include:
  - managerial grid
  - transactional analysis
  - role theory
  - assertiveness
  - ethical leading (pages 192–203).
- In the end, your effective leadership style will be the one that gets the results that you desire (page 203).

Skills checkout

The choice of what leadership style that you adopt isn't a straightforward or simple one. As such it will need you to continue to develop, refine and expand your individual 'bundle' of skills. If you think about what you've read you soon realise that these will include skills such as:

planning	thinking strategically
analysing	risk management
decision making	presenting and managing
prioritising	information
learning	communicating
managing conflict	influencing and persuading
monitoring	evaluating
problem solving	leading by example
obtaining/providing feedback	motivating
valuing and supporting	balancing competing needs
mentoring	empowering
learning	inspiring
involving others	building consensus

All of these are needed for Units B8 and B9 of the Providing Direction section of the UK National Occupational Standards for Management and Leadership.

How will we do it tomorrow?

In this chapter you'll look at the ways in which leaders and leadership might change in the near and distant future. First, you'll briefly remind yourself about some of the history of leading, then you'll move on to take a look at some of the new and recent changes to that process.

The changing face of leadership

At the beginning of this book (see Chapter 2 – What's it all about?), you saw that the idea of being a leader has been around for a long time. Despite this, the study of leaders and leadership didn't really get under way until the middle of the twentieth century. Since then, however, a considerable number of studies have been completed, almost all of which have been aimed at establishing the 'how and why' of leadership. These, together with the influence and effects of the tides and seasons of world affairs and several world and other wars, have led to significant changes in the way that we describe and understand leadership (see Table 2.1). This picture of the 'how and why' of leadership continues to evolve and flourish –

as also do our views of and opinions about the organisations in which that leading takes place.

So, let's move on to take a look at what's happening in the early twenty-first century and how that might influence the leadership of the future.

Organisational evolution

Earlier in this book (Chapter 2 – What's it all about?) you saw that the nature, culture, size and history of our organisations have all exerted a significant influence on the ways in which our theories and views about the nature of leadership have changed and evolved. Later (Chapter 8 – Where do you do it?) you read about the influences of your organisation's structure, mission, culture and attitude to profit-making as well as the culture of the nation or country in which it operates.

All of these and other influences continue to act upon our organisations. They do so at a time when changes in the 'world at large' have created a situation in which volatility, uncertainty, complexity and ambiguity are the new 'norms'. As a result a number of new ideas about our organisations have evolved.

Learning organisations

Peter Senge (see Further Information and Reading) tells us that a learning organisation is *'a group of people working together to collectively enhance their capacities to create results they really care about'*. You've already seen (Chapter 3 – Who's got the map?) the value of PESTLE and SWOT analyses – strategic planning tools that look, respectively, outward at the environment that surrounds your organisation or workgroup and inward at the organisation or workgroup itself.

A learning organisation takes this sort of examination a step further. For it uses continuous feedback. This is feedback that loops back from both the external environment and the organisation itself. It enables the organisation to detect its own errors and then quickly correct them. The learning organisation is said to be able to:

● 'unlearn' old beliefs
● remain open to new feedback
● limit or eliminate the effects of long-held beliefs.

Senge suggests that five key disciplines are key to this process:

● **Systems thinking** – you've already seen that organisations are complex webs of relationships, some of which are formal and 'hard', others of which are informal and 'soft'. Systems thinking enables these to be analysed and their problems found and eliminated.
● **Personal mastery** – a learning organisation can be described as the sum of individual learning and personal mastery as in the commitment made by all individual employees to the process of learning and personal development.
● **Mental models** – all organisations have a 'culture', a complex pattern of beliefs, values, rituals, myths and sentiments that are shared by the members of the organisation. Learning organisations have ways of examining, assessing and challenging these.
● **Shared vision** – a learning organisation's employees all share a common vision.
● **Team learning** – when this occurs, through dialogue and group discussion, individual learning accumulates and moves up to the larger and more productive team learning.

The benefits of being a learning organisation are said to be:

- higher levels of innovation
- enhanced competitiveness
- greater ability to respond to external pressures and changes
- better understanding of customer needs, and
- improved output quality and corporate image.

Networking organisations

Networks, in their simplest form, consist of people – as individuals or groups – who interact interdependently for a given purpose and over a given period of time. In the jargon of networking the individuals in a network are called 'nodes' and are connected (or 'tied') together by a wide range of interdependencies such as friendship, kinship, common interest, dislike, sexual relationships or commonality of beliefs. A network of organisations has a very similar structure except that its nodes are organisations. These are linked together in ways that aim to:

- enhance or optimise their interactions
- accomplish a common, overall goal.

A network like this can be seen to behave as a single, larger, unit or organisation. However, the organisations that make up the network are usually, though not always, independent of each other. There are three types of organisational network:

- **Internal networks** – these are loose associations of business units that are contained within a single organisation. They are, however, exposed to forces of the external market and may sell their products both inside and outside the parent organisation.

- **Stable networks** – these consist of a central organisation surrounded by other smaller organisations to which it outsources many of its operations. The relationship between the core organisation and its suppliers can be very close.
- **Dynamic networks** – these consist of temporary alliances of organisations with key skills organised around a lead, integrating or brokering organisation. Frequently used in the fashion industry bringing together manufacturers, designers and retailers.

The benefits of networking like this include:

- Speed of communication – rapid interchange of information takes place between the 'sharp-end' and the support units.
- Access to expertise – network members can tap into knowledge and expertise wherever it exists in the network.
- Resilience – a network has an ability to continue to operate even if some nodes fail.
- Responsiveness – networks are sensitive to and able to adapt to changes in the marketplace and the external environment.

Virtual organisations

These are organisations in which all (or almost all) interactions take place by electronic means. These interactions can be internal – as between business units, or external – as with customers and suppliers. In the purest form of the virtual organisation none of these meet each other – it's all electronic. Some virtual businesses actually operate solely in a virtual world – as in Second Life where virtual property, products and services are provided for virtual customers in a virtual world. Amazon – the online bookseller – was a virtual business pioneer. It delivers bookstore and, more recently, general store services solely through an online store presence. The benefits of a virtual organisation include its ability to:

- service a global marketplace
- quickly pool specialised knowledge and expert resources
- respond to rapidly changing needs, and
- provide increasingly 'niche' products and services.

Organisations as self-organising systems

At the extreme edge of current thinking about the ways and means of future organisations you'll find the idea of the organisation as a self-organising system. Self-organisation is the process where a structure or pattern appears in a system without being imposed by a central authority or external element. It's said that many biological systems display this characteristic. It's also an outcome or a part of what's called a complex adaptive system, a term created at the interdisciplinary Santa Fe Institute (see Further Information and Reading). Self-organising systems are described as being able to continually change their structure and internal processes as a response to feedback from the environment within which they exist. To survive, these self-organising systems need:

- strong or robust goals and purposes
- continual exchange of feedback with surroundings
- continual reference to a common set of values
- continual and shared dialogue about the system's current processes.

The leader of this type of organisation is described as placing a high value on communication and displaying a great deal of patience.

General views

Finally, other, more conventional, predictions tell us that the organisations of the future will be:

- facing increased levels of complexity
- flatter and more decentralised, with a top management that gets and gives more feedback with those at the 'sharp end'
- mindful of environments, changes, patterns and themes – able to reflect and learn from experience
- based on capability, so that the organisation is a means to an end rather than an end in itself
- strongly people-centric, with feedback systems that enable them to stay highly attuned and adaptive to the needs of all stakeholders.

People parts

At their core, all of our organisations are collections of interdependent people. You've already seen (see Chapter 9 – Who's following and why?) that the soft, informal and human side of your organisation is at least as powerful as its formal side. This soft side plays a significant role in what one researcher calls the psychological 'contract' that exists between an organisation and the people who work in it. This is a relationship that appears to be changing; people are looking for more meaning and purpose in their work; they expect to be valued for who they are as well as what they contribute to the aims and achievements of their organisation. Some of them even expect to have the opportunity to 'co-author' the aims and purpose of that organisation. Because of all of this it's not surprising to find that the range and number of views about the 'how and why' of people in our organisations has continued to expand.

Emotional intelligence

The study of what's now called 'emotional intelligence' dates to 1990 when two American university professors (John Mayer and Peter Salovey) published articles in two academic journals. The title of one of these papers was 'Emotional Intelligence'. These articles suggested that some people appeared to be better at identifying their own and other people's feelings and solving problems involving emotional issues. They also defined emotional intelligence as *'the ability to monitor one's own and others' feelings and emotions, to discriminate among them and to use this information to guide one's thinking and actions.'* Mayer and Salovey went on to propose a model of emotional intelligence that contained four key abilities:

- identify and perceive emotions
- reason using emotions
- understand emotion, and
- manage emotions.

These were said to be arranged so that there was a progression from the lowest level – the ability to perceive and understand emotion – up to the highest level, which is the 'conscious, reflective regulation of emotion'. Mayer and Salovey went on to develop two tests that aimed to measure emotional intelligence. But the publication, in 1996, of a highly popular book by psychologist and science writer Daniel Goleman (see Further Information and

Reading) further popularised and expanded the idea of emotional intelligence. Both Salovey and Goleman went on to write separately on their individual views about the relevance and value of emotional intelligence to leadership. Goleman, for example, writing in a *Harvard Business Review* article entitled 'Primal Leadership – The Hidden Driver of Great Performance' went on to claim that a leader's emotional 'style' drives everyone else's moods and behaviours through a neurological process called 'mood contagion' that's akin to the 'smile and the whole world smiles with you' process. However, Salovey (see Further Information and Reading) argues that good decisions require both emotions and logic and that it's the integration of the rational and emotional 'styles' that's important for successful leadership.

Motivation 1.0, 2.0 and 3.0

You've seen earlier in this book (see Chapter 9 – Who's following and why?) that motivation is a key factor when it comes to both leading and following. In that chapter you read about the outlines of several theories about what does and doesn't motivate us. Daniel Pink (see Further Information and Reading) classifies these theories and their precursors as:

- Motivation 1.0 theories – that were all about survival, and
- Motivation 2.0 theories – that identified people's responses to rewards.

Pink then goes on to tell us about Motivation 3.0. This is based on the ideas of Edward Deci and Richard Ryan, American professors who developed the Self Determination Theory (SDT) of motivation. This theory has the idea of autonomy – acting from choice rather than acting in response to external pressures – at its core. It also says the autonomy, together with competence and relatedness represent the three innate psychological needs that we all have. Satisfy them, we're told, and we'll be 'motivated, productive and happy'. Fail to do that and our motivation, productivity and happiness will nose-dive. But this autonomy needs to be focused and it's suggested that the focus of our individual autonomy should be on the four t's:

- **task** – such as in Google where engineers spend one day a week on 'side-projects'
- **time** – such as work being about results rather than 'clock-watching' or putting in time
- **technique** – individual authority to respond to customer needs rather than to pre-ordained scripts, and
- **team** – such as the small self-organised teams with almost no budget or authority that try, and often succeed, to change something.

By now you might be thinking that you've met all this before under the guise of empowerment. However, Pink tells us that Motivation 3.0 is different – it's about engagement and that, as we saw way back at the beginning of this book (see Chapter 1 – Who is this book for?) produces results.

Theory U and Theory T

Another variation on the alphabetic school of motivation theories has been identified by former management consultant Matthew Stewart. Writing in the April 2010 issue of the *strategy + business* magazine to mark the fifteenth anniversary of Douglas McGregor's Theory X and Theory Y (see Chapter 9 – Who's following and why?), Stewart tells us about Theory U and Theory T.

Theory U – for Utopian – assumes that all conflicts have their roots in misunderstandings. So, the theory says, get rid of the false assumptions and subsequent conflictful attitudes and people will return to a 'natural state of peace'. However, Theory T – for Tragic – assumes that conflict is built into the 'warp and weft' of human interactions. Peace is, therefore, a temporary condition, and whether or not it survives doesn't depend on people's attitudes but on the 'system' of their relations. Both of these theories emphasise the importance of 'trust'. Theory U, for example, says that trust starts to accumulate when you show people that you trust them by relaxing your control over them. Theory T, however, says you build trust by demonstrating that things are under control — by creating a system in which rewards and punishments are doled out.

Gender differences

Not all of the factors that are influencing leadership in the twenty-first century are positive or good. Harvard University's Barbara Kellerman tells us that as far as leadership is concerned, women – at least in America, the home of the corporation – are hardly any better off than they were a generation ago. Here are some of the facts that she cites to illustrate that situation:

- 3 per cent of Fortune 500 companies have women CEOs (2009).
- 6 per cent of the 100 top tech companies are headed by women (2010).
- 15 per cent of members of Fortune 500 boards are women (2009).
- 16.8 per cent of members of the US Congress are women (2010).
- 14.5 per cent of 249 mayors of US cities with populations over 100,000 are women (2010).
- 21 per cent of non-profit-making organisations with budgets greater than $25 million are headed by women (2010).

- 5 per cent of generals in the US Army are women (2008).
- 8 per cent of admirals in the US Navy are women (2009).
- 19 per cent of senior faculty at the Harvard Business School are women (2009–10).

In the UK, a similar pattern emerges when you look at the women-in-power 'milestones' that the UK Government records on its equality website:

1907	First woman councillor elected in Britain
1918	Women over 30 have the right to vote
1918	Women can stand as Members of Parliament
1919	First woman to take a seat in Parliament
1928	Vote given to women on same terms as men
1958	Women can sit in House of Lords
1976	First Asian woman councillor elected
1979	UK's first woman Prime Minister
1981	First woman Leader of the House of Lords
1984	First black female mayor
1987	First black woman MP
1990	First female Asian peer
1997	Proportion of women MPs doubles to reach 18 per cent
1998	First Muslim woman in the House of Lords
1999	First Asian female MEP
2003	First black woman appointed to Cabinet
2003	First black woman Leader of the House of Lords
2007	First black woman Attorney General.

It's reported that, in 2007, only 22 per cent of the senior management posts in the UK's FTSE 350 companies were held by women. In the same year it was reported that the average salary for male white-collar workers in China was 44,000 yuan compared with 28,700 yuan for female white-collar workers. The United Nations is reported as having concluded that women often experience a 'glass ceiling' and that there are no societies in which women enjoy the same opportunities as men. Recent research (CMI 2010 National Management Salary Survey) has revealed that:

- the average UK male manager currently earns £10,071 more than a female manager
- female workforce redundancies over the past 12 months were 50 per cent higher than male redundancies (female 4.5 per cent; male 3 per cent)
- 7.7 per cent of female directors voluntarily left their posts in the past year compared with just 3.6 per cent of male directors.

The CMI's Head of Policy, Petra Wilton, tells us that: 'Girls born this year will face the probability of working for around 40 years in the shadow of unequal pay.' Table 11.1 lists some of the current laws that make gender discrimination illegal.

Table 11.1: Gender discrimination legislation

Australia	Sex Discrimination Act 1984
Canada	Ontario Human Rights Code 1962 Canadian Human Rights Act 1977
United Kingdom	Equal Pay Act 1970 Sex Discrimination Act 1975 Human Rights Act 1998
United States	Equal Pay Act 1963 Title VII of Civil Rights Act 1964 Pregnancy Discrimination Act 1978

Twenty-first-century leadership

You saw in Chapter 2 – What's it all about? – that leadership is an elusive, almost slippery idea that has changed and evolved to meet the demands of history. So far, the twenty-first century has done little to limit that ability to change and, as a result, it's not surprising to find that further ideas about leadership have evolved.

Value-based leadership

You've already seen, in Chapter 10 – How do you do it? – that ethics are an integral part of your leading style. These ethics are closely related to your individual values and as such they will influence or lead to what is called value-based leadership.

Value-based leadership is described as being an attitude rather than a theory. As such it encompasses the whole organisation – its people, its objectives and its processes. It's also said to have the following characteristics:

- integrity
- vision
- trust
- listening
- respect for and inclusion of followers, and
- clear thinking about beliefs.

Value-based leaders are said to lead by example rather than by the use of those good old standbys, power, manipulation and coercion. Ambitious and, some would argue, idealistic words and phrases such as liberty, equality and natural justice are used in describing the beliefs of such leaders. These leaders face the challenge of leading change both morally and, in process terms, effectively and, like the servant leaders that you'll soon read about, they aim to answer and realise the needs and the aspirations of their followers.

Servant leadership

When you think about the sort of things that are happening in the world today you shouldn't be too surprised when you find that there's an idea about leadership that's the exact opposite of the authoritarian, autocratic or directive style (see Chapter 2 – What's it all about?). This – the servant style of leadership – was first identified by Robert Greenleaf as far back as 1970. Since then, the concept – which is based on an ethical perspective of leadership that identifies key moral behaviours that leaders must continuously demonstrate – has continued to grow in popularity. The servant leader is said to serve the people he/she leads, an action that implies that employees or followers are an end in themselves rather than a means towards the endpoint of organisational purpose or the 'bottom line'. The dimensions of the framework for this sort of leadership are said to include: listening, empathy, healing, awareness, persuasion, conceptualisation, foresight, stewardship, commitment to people's growth and community building. Greenleaf stated (see Further Information and Reading) that *'caring for persons, the more able and the less able serving each other, is the rock upon which a good society is built'*. He also went on to say that the servant-leader style of leadership – which can be described as a philosophy rather than a theory – has its roots in the individual feeling of wanting to serve others. It's fairly obvious that leading that's driven by this need will be quite different from the sort of leadership that's driven by personal ambition. Nevertheless, it's argued that blends of these two can exist.

Learning leaders

Earlier in this chapter you read about the power and influence of the learning organisation. Peter Senge tells us that, in this sort of organisation, traditional leadership is no longer effective and that what's needed is a 'new' view of leadership – one that's focused on 'subtler and more important tasks'.

These tasks involve a leader in acting as:

- a 'designer'
- a 'steward', and
- a 'teacher'.

The first of these – acting as a designer – involves identifying and sharing the organisation's governing ideas – its purpose, vision and core values. The role then moves on to identify and implement the organisation's policies, strategies and systems. When acting as a steward, the leader makes a commitment to, and takes responsibility for, the learning organisation's vision. However, stewardship is not the same as ownership and the leader's task is to manage that vision for the benefit of others. Doing this will involve learning to listen to other people's visions and changing your own vision where necessary. Finally, when acting as a teacher, the leader doesn't teach people in the conventional sense – he or she fosters learning, for everyone and throughout the whole organisation.

Tribal leadership

David Logan (see Further Information and Reading) has a view of leadership that's based on the idea that all organisations are made up of tribes. These tribes are described as naturally occurring groups that are larger than teams and typically consist of between 20 and 150 people. These people are said to be bound together by familiarity and shared work. Logan argues that these tribes exist in one of five 'culture states' that, in terms of rising productivity and effectiveness, can be 'stacked' one on top of another. One of the core differences between these stages is that they use language in quite different ways:

- **Stage 1** – members say 'Life sucks' and see the world as unfair, are alienated from each other and have undermining relationships. Consists of around 2 per cent of the population and are typically found in prisons and gangs.
- **Stage 2** – members say 'My life sucks' and see themselves as powerless and oppressed victims with ineffective relationships. Consists of around 25 per cent of the population.
- **Stage 3** – members say 'I'm great, because you're not!' with one tribe member being typically dominant over others with conflictful relationships that are developed for their usefulness. Consists of around 48 per cent of the population, most of us live here.
- **Stage 4** – members say 'We are great (because they're not)!' and cooperate around a common goal and see their place in the world as meaningful. Stable partnerships exist and are seen to be important. Consists of around 22 per cent of the population and can do remarkable things.
- **Stage 5** – members say 'Life is Great!' and see their place in the world as intrinsically meaningful with stable partnerships and relationships being very important. Consists of around 2 per cent of the population.

The job of a tribal leader is to move the tribe up through these stages. To do this they have to be knowledgeable about and fluent in the language of each and all of the stages. This shift occurs one stage at a time and stages are not skipped. Shifting up a stage involves moving many people forward, individually, by helping them to use a different language, and to shift their behaviour accordingly. Studies indicate that significant productivity increases (at least 30 per cent) when a leader manages a shift from Stage 3 to Stage 4.

Facebook leaders

Seth Godin (see Further Information and Reading) has another view of tribal leadership – one that starts from the idea that, to turn an ordinary informal group of people, first, into a tribe and then into a movement, only takes two things:

- a shared interest, and
- a way to communicate.

Things like the internet, blogs, Twitter and Facebook mean that the communicating bit is a lot easier and faster these days. As a result, all sorts of messages pass via these media from leader to tribe, tribe to leader, tribe member to tribe member and from tribe member to outsider. As a result, ideas spread – like wildfire if the tribe has a common story about who they are and what sort of future they're trying to build. Great tribal leaders, Godin says, 'create movements by empowering the tribe to communicate'. What happens here is that a shared interest gets transformed – into a shared goal driven by a passionate desire for change. So, whether you do or don't Tweet, the message is simple – a movement , or to put it another way, the process of converting your vision into a reality, is about communication. Godin goes on to say that creating a movement means doing five things and following six principles, as listed below:

Things to do	Principles to follow
1. Publish, give away and broadcast a manifesto.	A. Be transparent and honest.
2. Make it easy for followers to connect with you.	B. Don't forget that your movement is bigger than you.
3. Make it easy for followers to connect with each other.	C. When movements grow, they thrive.
4. Realise that money isn't the point – it's an enabling mechanism.	D. Movement objectives are clearest when compared with the status quo.
5. Track and monitor your progress.	E. Exclude outsiders.
	F. Building your followers up is better than tearing others down.

Shared leadership

Traditional leadership has always been a top-down affair in which a single leader makes key decisions, motivates, creates visions and inspires. But shared leadership tells us that leadership can be shared and enacted by several people simultaneously. This sort of leadership is sometimes called distributed leadership.

Getting this sort of leadership to work is neither simple nor easy. If it's going to be successful then five things must happen:

1. Power must be distributed in a balanced way.
2. There must be a shared purpose or goal.
3. Responsibility for the work of the group must be shared.
4. Everyone in the partnership must recognise, embrace and respect the differences in skills, knowledge and ability that exist within the group.

5. This partnership must work in complex, real-world situations.

Distributed leadership does have some of the characteristics of a team that manages or controls (see Chapter 8 – Where do you do it?) and its main advantage is the sort of 2+2=5 synergy that has the potential to happen when people work well together.

Chapter checklist

In this chapter you've taken a look at the ways in which leading and leadership might change in the future. Use the list below to check where you've got to. If you've missed something or don't understand it go back to the page given and read through it again.

- New ideas about our organisations include:
  - learning organisations (page 208)
  - networking organisations (page 210)
  - virtual organisations (page 211)
  - organisations as self-organising systems (see page 212).
- Predictions suggest that the organisations of our future will be:
  - facing more complexity
  - flatter and more decentralised
  - mindful of environments, changes, patterns and themes
  - based on capability
  - strongly people-centric (page 213).
- The changing 'people-parts' of leadership include:
  - emotional intelligence (page 214)
  - Motivation 3.0 (page 215).
- Women are still finding it difficult to achieve significant leadership roles (page 217).

- New or developing ideas about leadership include:
  - value-based leadership (page 220)
  - servant leadership (page 221)
  - learning leadership (page 222)
  - tribal leadership (page 222)
  - Facebook leadership (page 224)
  - shared leadership (page 225).

Skills checkout

Adapting to the new ways and means of leadership in the twenty-first century will be demanding. As such it will need you to continue to develop, refine and expand your individual 'bundle' of skills. If you think about what you've read you soon realise that these will include skills such as:

planning	thinking strategically
risk management	communicating
consulting	influencing and persuading
monitoring	evaluating
problem solving	leading by example
obtaining/providing feedback	motivating
valuing and supporting	managing conflict
following	balancing competing needs
mentoring	empowering
learning	inspiring
involving others	

These are needed for all of the units of the Providing Direction section of the UK National Occupational Standards for Management and Leadership.

12

The Companion Interview: Michael, Lord Bichard KCB on leading people

The following interview with Lord Bichard, when he was Rector of The University of the Arts London, was conducted by Ed Peppitt, author of *Six of the Best* (Hodder).

His previous roles include Chief Executive of two Local Authorities and the Government's Benefits Agency, and Permanent Secretary of the Department for Education and Employment. He also chaired the Legal Services Commission and the Soham Inquiry. He became Rector of The University of the Arts London in September 2001. Lord Bichard was created a life peer on 24 March 2010 and currently serves as a Senior Fellow (previously Executive Director) of the Institute for Government and as Chair of the Design Council.

In his interview, Lord Bichard (then Sir Michael Bichard) focuses firmly on the importance of values, passion and communication in leading and inspiring people in any organisation.

Ed Peppitt writes:

There is an awful lot written about how to lead people. Entire sections in the bookshop are dedicated to leadership, motivation and the distinction between managing and leading a team of people.

My brief was to meet and talk to someone who had led teams of people effectively throughout their career. Who better qualified than Sir Michael Bichard, who as Chief Executive of the Benefits Agency had led a team of 65,000 staff? If anyone could explain what leading people was about, it would be him.

As I arrived at the University of the Arts London, where Sir Michael is Rector, I read the Chartered Management Institute's own summary of what leading people means:

> **'The increasing role of values, communication and interpersonal relationships have emphasised the growing complexity of leadership in today's dynamic workplaces. But leadership is not just expected from those at the top of an organisation. Increasingly, it is a challenge for all, especially as many organisations have become flatter and less hierarchical.'**

Would Sir Michael agree with this statement? Just what are the skills that make up a good leader? How should successful leadership be defined – simply by the goals achieved by an organization, or is there more to it than that? Does good leadership depend on the decisions and judgements made by an individual, or the circumstances they are made in? I jotted these questions down, along with many others, as I sat down in Sir Michael's office.

Vision, values and taking ownership

I began the interview by reading the quotation from the Chartered Management Institute. Did Sir Michael Bichard agree that leadership was all about values, communication and interpersonal relationships?

It is certainly one way of covering the issue. I think as a leader, particularly in large organisations, my aim has always been to try to create a sense of purpose and direction. I think there are two particular things that enable you to do that. One is to get some ownership for a clear business vision – you need to know where the business or organisation is going. The other is to get a sense of ownership for a clear set of values. For me, values have always been as important as the business vision, because values are about behaviour. So what I am trying to do is not just get clarity about where the business is going, but also about how the people in the business are going to behave together.

So leadership is about vision and values?

Yes. And ownership, because lots of organisations say they've got a vision, and some say they've got values. But if people in the organisation don't recognise that they have some ownership of the vision and values, then they don't have any effect on the way the organisation works. However, if you get it right it can be a driving force. When I was in the Benefits Agency, we did a lot of work on the values there. We had just three or four values. You could go to any office in the country and they would tell you what the values were. Then gradually you could see people interpreting the values in their own way. For example, one of the values was customer service and quality. They began to develop their own take on that, using their own initiatives. But basically you have still got to have clarity and ownership of vision and values at the outset.

So it was a good thing that people were interpreting the values in their own way?

Oh yes, absolutely. The most exciting thing of all in leadership, I think, is to get to the point where people are using their own initiative to deliver. They won't always do it in exactly the way you would have done, but I think one of the tasks of leaders sometimes is just to step back and stop making people do things the way you would do them.

You mentioned the Benefits Agency earlier, and I read that you had overall control of 65,000 people. With an organisation with such a massive head count, where did you begin, how did you start?

It was being set up as a new organisation, so it was the biggest of the government's Next Step agencies. The staff came from the DSS, the Department of Social Security. They were being set up as a separate entity with its own kind of identity, its own pride. So I had an opportunity not to start completely afresh, but to think radically about what kind of organisation it wanted to be.

At the time, the staff had been taught that customers weren't that important, and that quality wasn't that important. This was an opportunity to say that customer service and quality were both very important. A lot of people in the organisation just wanted to be liberated, just wanted to be told by the leader that actually these things really did matter and they could then get on and use their initiative to improve the quality.

I can see how, as a new department, the vision was there from the outset. But what about the values? Where did they come from? Were they your values?

I think any leader has a set of values. I think what you need to do is to take your values to the organisation and make them clear. At your initial job interview, if necessary. Because I think if you go to an organisation where your values are not welcome, you may get through the interview, but actually what you will end up doing is having hell for four or five years because you will constantly be fighting a group of people in an organisation that don't share your basic values.

I have basic values around the way I treat people and respect people. I have basic values around what I think of clients and customers, and how I expect people to be treated and the importance of service. I try to make those clear at the outset. I think when you then engage with the organisation you probably adjust and adapt your values, so you may express them in slightly different ways. You may emphasise one of your values at a particular time and emphasise another at another time, but if you are a leader trying to lead an organisation in a way which is not compatible with your basic values, then it is not going to work.

I think leaders have to be natural. They have to be themselves. I mean, there are different sorts of leaders, some of them are introverts, some of them are extroverts – but the leaders I have always respected are the people who are being themselves. You can't be yourself if you are trying to pretend that the values of the organisation are your values, or vice versa.

So if you had been head-hunted, or you are applying for a job of some sort of leadership role in an organisation, and you know perfectly well that their values aren't yours, what should you do?

You don't go there. I think one of the other things that all of the leaders I respect have had is a passion and a belief in what they are doing in the organisation, in the product, in the service.

I always say to young people, on speech days and at degree ceremonies, for God's sake don't get yourself into a position where you don't feel passionate about what you are doing. Because again, it is not something you can pretend. People know whether you believe in what you are doing in the organisation. If they don't believe that their leader is passionate and has belief, then what chance do you have that they will?

Is that part of the difference, do you think, between a manager and a leader?

Everyone always asks me, what is the difference between management and leadership? I am not a great reader, but the best definition I know is by John Kotter, an American academic, who talks about *management* in terms of planning, budgeting, monitoring, identifying issues, resolving issues and evaluating. By contrast, *leadership* is about creating this sense of purpose and direction. It's about getting ownership, getting people aligned to it, and it is actually about getting people to believe they can achieve it. And that's very different. I think you can sustain an organisation in reasonably stable times through good management. But transforming an organisation takes real leadership, and not leadership just at the top of the organisation: it is about getting leadership right the way through the organisation. I talk to people who may only have four or five people working for them, but they are leading that team – and how effective that team is depends very much upon the quality of their leadership.

And what's the process for identifying potential leaders of smaller teams throughout an organisation, and then getting them to take ownership of the values and the direction?

You have got to spend a lot of time getting people involved in the discussion about the vision and the values. In this university, about a year ago, we spent several months talking to as many staff as we could about what our strategy should be in the medium term, and what kind of place we wanted this university to be. A university is not the easiest place to do that because people are not used to that kind of debate. Many just want to teach and research, and leave the management issues to others. But it was a really positive exercise.

That's exactly what we did in the Benefits Agency as well. I spent the first six months in the Benefits Agency visiting and talking to people personally about the values we wanted, what we believed in, the things that would make us a successful organisation. That's part of the process of getting ownership. I mean, if people across the organisation don't own the vision, then it is not going to happen. They won't all take ownership, but you have to get a critical mass.

That is very interesting. And, from your experience, does that process tend to identify people who realise that their values don't match up to those of the organisation that they work for?

Absolutely. I always take the view that if someone leaves the organisation, particularly if they are in a senior position, then that's a failure, in that you want people to be part of the organisation. But there are clearly times when there is a mismatch, and when you have to part company with someone. When you get to that point, I have never seen any reason to treat individuals with anything less than dignity. After all, some people have been brought up to work in a particular way for 25 years, because that's what's been wanted from them in the past. It would be very arrogant of someone to come in and say, 'Well actually I want to do something completely different and we don't need you any more'. You need to try to give people the opportunity to be a part of the change – but if they can't, then you need to help them to find something else.

Communication

I was starting to build a clear picture in my mind of Sir Michael Bichard's approach to leading teams. Sharing the organisation's vision, and its values, forms the basis of this approach. But sharing the vision and the values only benefits an organisation if its people are given genuine ownership of them. That means that an organisation must involve its people from the outset, rather than simply hand them the latest strategic direction policy document.

I understood the theory, but how do you communicate or share a vision throughout an organisation, particularly one the size of, for example, the Benefits Agency? I needed to probe deeper.

So, if we consider the vision for a moment, how is it communicated across this university? Or throughout the Benefits Agency? Is it simply a case of talking to people, as you mentioned, or are you publicising it in any other way?

I think the way in which you communicate effectively depends upon the size of the organisation. It is a bit like talking to an audience. If I am talking to an audience of ten people then I adopt a very different style than if I am talking to an audience of 500 people. If you are running the Benefits Agency with 500 offices and 65,000 staff, you know you are going to adopt a different strategy for communication than if you are running a much smaller organisation. I don't think there's a science. I think you have got to keep changing the way in which you communicate, because communications can become very routine and then people don't listen.

So you have got to adopt a whole panoply of different strategies. They need to include some personal visibility, and that's not easy when you are dealing with 500 offices. I've seen people torture themselves running national organisations by trying always to be up front and spending their whole week on a train. You can't do that, but you have got to show some personal visibility. Fortunately, with technology now you can do it in all sorts of other ways, such as emails and websites. I used to put my diary on the web so that people could see what I was doing for the next couple of weeks and what I thought were important issues. For a smaller organisation, I would adopt a rather more intimate style, such as coffee mornings, tea-breaks, lunches. I used to advertise that I would be in the building, and available, at ten o'clock on Wednesdays if people wanted to come and have a chat.

I think that there are two important things in communication. One is, it isn't just about telling, it really is about listening. The other thing is getting the balance right between being consistent without being rigid. People don't want the message to change fundamentally every week, particularly if you are trying to change an organisation. So the fundamental message has got to be consistent. If you say that this organisation stands for caring for its staff, the quality of its service, the way it treats its customers and the value for money it provides, then you do not change those fundamental messages. Otherwise people just get totally confused, or de-energised. That's a mistake that a lot of managers and leaders make – they are constantly giving out different messages. So it's important to be consistent.

But if you are listening, then you can't be rigid, partly because you are learning things all the time, and partly because there are things going on which you must adapt to. So you have got to be flexible whilst remaining consistent.

Yes, I can see the importance of communication, particularly in a vast organisation such as the

Benefits Agency. But how do you set in motion the structures and methodologies that enable you to listen to the issues and concerns of so many different people?

I think you can start with some of the mechanisms I have talked a bit about already. It is not rocket science, frankly. If you are genuine about wanting to do it, there are all sorts of ways in which you can communicate with people. I think the question is whether the individual, the leader, has actually got the ability to communicate, really communicate, including listening and talking, with different people in different parts of the organisation – put them at their ease, convince them that you really are listening and that you want to hear what they say, understanding, trying to get into their shoes. For me, communication is about trying to get in the shoes of the people you are talking to on the front line in the Toxteth Benefit Office. What kind of pressures are they are facing?

That sounds like rapport-building?

Yes, I think the rapport is putting people at their ease. I used to watch some permanent secretaries doing visits, and they would make a great thing about how they were in touch with the staff. Yet they would actually take four or five people with them and descend on an office, and everyone there was on edge. It was a sort of inspection tour. And you come away from that, and you haven't learned anything. People don't tell you what really is bothering them because they don't think you want to hear it.

What people really want is to be reassured that everything is OK. But what you have to do sometimes, if you want to improve the quality of service and if you really care about that as a leader, is to find out what's not working very well. And sometimes you discover that something you have suggested is part of the reason why it isn't working very well. You have to put people sufficiently at their ease for them to be able to say, 'Look, what really is getting us down is this'. But too many leaders don't want to hear that.

The Benefits Agency was a good example. For the first two years in the Benefits Agency, there was so much anger in that organisation that when you went to visit Grimsby on a Friday, they wanted to sit you down and just tell you how angry they were. And sometimes I came away feeling hugely depressed and the only way I could keep going was to recognise that they thought I might do something about it, otherwise they wouldn't waste their time telling me. With some leaders, the staff just didn't think they were going to do anything, so they didn't waste their breath.

That is a stark picture. In those circumstances, did you feel that it was your responsibility to take away their anger? Or accept it but try to do something about it?

Well two things really. One is, if people tell you things that can be fixed, you fix them. You make sure that someone goes back and tells them what you've done, otherwise you have even lower credibility with them. I used to do phone-ins, which is slightly old technology now, but I would set aside a day when everyone would know that they could ring me and complain, or make points, and we had an arrangement whereby they always got a reply within three weeks. You have got to make sure you go back and respond to their concerns.

The other thing to realise is that sometimes people just want to get something off their chests. Most people don't expect miracles, but they do think that the leader ought to be interested enough to let them let off steam from time to time. You have got to be resilient. Sometimes you have got to take that on the chin.

I believe that leaders earn huge credibility if people believe that they are trying to get rid of some of the obstacles that are stopping them doing a good job. And partly this is about finding out just what *is* stopping people doing a good job, because most people want to do a good job. They don't want to come and be a pain in the neck and they don't want to work for an organisation that is unsuccessful. So if you can get across to people that you are really trying to find out what the obstacles are and that you want to do something about them, then they'll listen to you.

Motivation and creating energy

I was intrigued by the idea that a leader earns huge credibility by trying to get rid of some of the obstacles that are stopping people doing a good job. The combination of listening to what your people have to say, and then doing something about the things that stand in their way, is clearly empowering. Communication at this level is persuasive, but what else must a leader do to motivate a team? Having read so much about motivation, I found Sir Michael's response both challenging and refreshing.

I was going to ask you about motivating a team and motivating employees, and it sounds as if the process you have just described is the key?

I find that 'motivating' is not a word I warm to, really. In a way I find it slightly condescending, as if you are manipulating people. The thing I am quite interested in, and have been for a while now, is creating energy, which is a different way of putting it. I think that one of the things that leaders can do most of all is to create and enhance energy in organisations, and it is one of the big distinctions, I think, between successful and unsuccessful leaders. I have seen people in leadership positions who stifle creativity and energy. I have visited many schools and workplaces in my time, and you don't need to be there very long to work out whether or not it is a place that has got buzz, energy, creativity, passion, or whether or not it is a really great place to be. Usually the reason for that is the person who is leading the team, the place, the school. So I think leaders need to think a lot more than they do about how you create energy.

I think one of the ways you create energy is to get rid of some of the obstacles. Every organisation has obstacles. Sometimes there are an excessive number of meetings, or a paper culture. In the Benefits Agency, there were endless audit checks. Everything that was done in that organisation was checked by someone else. Every single decision. And this meant that the people who took the decisions thought that they weren't being valued because they were always going to be checked. And I thought, why on earth are we doing this? So we introduced a random checking procedure which achieved what we wanted but didn't involve quite such a bureaucratic process. So you try to get rid of the things that are concealing the energy, you try to get rid of the dysfunction.

A lot of leaders, I think, try to turn their back on some of the disagreements that are going on within the organisation, either with individuals or between workplaces. But doing that drags down the energy levels of the organisation.

So get rid of the things that conceal the energy and then try to think about ways in which you can create energy. One example is the way in which you personally go about things. For instance, if someone comes in here with an idea, you can either send them out feeling full of energy and enthusiasm, or you can tell them all the reasons why it won't happen. Or you can tell them 'We tried that in 1986', or 'We haven't got enough money', or 'Sorry, I'm really busy today' or 'It's good in theory but it's not going to work in practice' – you get the idea. If they go out and feel de-motivated, they will tell everybody else. They won't come to you with new ideas. The organisation has lost a pocket of energy and has replaced it with someone who is just going to serve their time. So I think the way in which the leader behaves has a huge impact on whether the organisation is passionate and has got energy.

That sounds great in theory. But if someone walks through your door here with an absolutely ridiculous idea in your opinion, what do you do then?

Well it depends on how ridiculous it is. I mean if someone comes through the door and has an idea which I think is silly, I would never say, 'That's a stupid idea'. What I would say is, 'Let's talk about it a bit more. How's it actually going to work in practice? How much is it going to cost? How is it going to fit in with some of the other things we are doing at the moment?' And you may well come to the conclusion, hopefully with that person, that this particular idea isn't going to work terribly well, but you have still sent them away knowing that you listened to them. It may not be a long conversation, but you can send them away with a sense that you were interested enough to have the conversation, and that if they had another idea they would bring it to you, rather than having demeaned them to the point where they would never come to you again.

The importance of teams

So rather than talking about motivating an individual person or motivating an individual team, it sounds to me as if the passion and the energy become infectious.

I think they do, and that's a reason why the snowball effect is important, because you have got to have the passion, you have got to have the energy, and your team around you have got to have it too. We haven't talked about teams, and I think one of the great skills of the most effective leaders is to get really effective teams around them.

So it's the recruitment of teams that is important?

Yes, recruit where you can, and gradually, if you take on a team that's already established then there will be changes over time, inevitably, and you have got to try to get around you a team that shares the values and the vision and really lives them. It's a bit of a cliché, but what the organisation is always doing is watching that team and seeing whether or not they are reflecting what you say the organisation is about, and how passionate they are. If they see that there are disagreements on fundamental issues, or people are talking down what you are trying to do behind your back, and you are not doing anything about it, then they assume that you are not serious and that the organisation is not serious. So getting a really strong team around you is very important.

How does that process begin?

If you are going into a ready-made team, it begins with an assessment of the people that are there. You need to be clear about where you are going and what kind of organisation you want to be, and you need to make it clear that you are going to do that together, and you are going to involve the organisation in it. Naturally, it may be that during the course of this process, one or two people don't share that vision or want to move on. Inevitably some people retire. Some people move on because they want to get promotion. There will be recruiting opportunities, and you have got to be clear about how you want to use those opportunities.

A great example was when we merged the departments for Education and Employment. It was a one-off opportunity really, so we took the decision that everyone was going to apply for the jobs, because everyone had to be sure that this was an honest process, and that no one was going to get the job just because they happened to have been in Education rather than Employment, or Employment rather than Education. The civil service often misses that kind of opportunity, because it doesn't have regard to attitudes, achievements or values – it appoints people on the basis of the jobs they have had in the past. I don't think that's enough. So we were pretty careful about the kind of people we appointed to that new board. Then we got one or two non-executive board members in as well, with the right set of skills, and the result was a fantastic board. As the leader of that board, your effectiveness is multiplied a thousand-fold because you have got eight or nine people there sharing the values, taking them through the organisation. It's a fantastic feeling.

So when you have a good leader of a team or a department, are you tempted to leave them alone?

I often say that there's always enough going wrong in any organisation not to waste your time interfering with people who are getting it right. So I think you are right. If I look back at some of the best people I have worked with, why would I want to second-guess every decision they were making? But I can be pretty interventionist if someone isn't getting it right!

Let's talk about that for a minute. Things aren't going right. Do you replace the leader?

Well, first you have got to have certain things in place. We have talked about the importance of vision and values. I think there is a clear sense of priorities in an organisation which you only get through a decent business plan. When I came to the university, there was no business plan process at all. There was a budget and target numbers for recruiting students, and that was about it. We have got six colleges here, and that was about the extent of business planning. Now we have a business plan process. It has credibility. I meet with the management teams of each of the colleges twice a year and I review how they are doing against their key priorities and against any other issues that have come up during the course of the year. We take those meetings very seriously. The meetings will be two or three hours long. I used to do it in the Department and at the Benefits Agency, and obviously I meet the senior managers pretty regularly apart from those meetings.

So to be clear about whether or not a college is performing well, or whether the leader of that college is performing well, I think my first task is to support the leader and look at ways in which we can help and identify if there are issues that can be resolved. But as we said, there are occasions when you get to the point where you think that the person just can't hack it, they are not going to be able to turn this round. If that's the case, your responsibility is to the college, to the organisation, and to the rest of the staff. You can't ignore the fact that the individual is damaging all of that, and so then I think you do have to look for ways in which you can respectfully part company and move on to something else.

You mentioned the business planning process a few minutes ago. Is it the role or the responsibility of the leader to develop the business plan?

Well I did, because that was a particular need that I felt we had and there was no one else who was going to do it. I think leadership is sometimes about adapting to different situations. For example, I was here with one of my chief executives just before you came in, and we were having a discussion about the extent to which he was 'hands-on'. We agreed that he was probably more hands-on than he would like to be. I was saying that I think sometimes that's inevitable. In the same way, I think that the business planning element here was inevitable and I've had to spend quite a lot of time on what is not strategic management, but operational management, because the skills weren't here. It was an important part of getting the university heading in the right direction. So I think you have got to be a bit flexible.

I would like to spend a little less time on business planning now, and spend more time on external relations and fund-raising, because the future of the university depends upon us getting more money which isn't government-related. So that's a new leadership task, in a way. You have got to be flexible.

Leadership across different organisations

Are the principles of leadership the same, regardless of the organisation?

Yes I think they are. I think the core of leadership is about people, but I think you have got to be sensitive to the history, the traditions, the customs and the practice of your organisation. I don't believe you can just go in headlong and impose your particular style on an organisation. One of the reasons I came here was that I wanted to try my leadership style in a different setting with different people – in this case, creatives, artists and designers.

Regardless of the organisation, though, one of the most difficult times for a leader is the first six months in a new organisation.

Why do you think that is?

Because on the one hand you have to go through that stage of listening and learning about the organisation, and quickly understanding the things that aren't working, as well as the things that it really feels passionate about. You have to make sure you don't step on a landmine. And so, in that sense, it is a time when you should be stepping back and listening.

But it is also the most powerful time you will ever get in the organisation, because people will listen to what you have to say. They will try to interpret you, and you can send out the most powerful signals and messages in that first six months. For example, I'm not hierarchical, I am not status-conscious, and I wanted to get that message across to people. This university, when I came here, was very status-conscious and hierarchical. If you want to break that quickly, then that's the time to do it.

So you have got to balance those two things, and I think often what I try to do is to do some of my listening and learning before I even join an organisation. It's not just by talking to people in the organisation, either. Some of the most insightful comments about an organisation come from people who are outside it, and who deal with it.

So it's important to do a lot of that learning, so that when you are in the building you actually know what the messages are that you want to send to that organisation. My messages here are around, 'We're here to deliver a top-class service to clients that we really care about – in this case students. I really care about results and outcomes. I am not someone who gets terribly uptight about processes. Sometimes processes are important, but by and large I don't mind an unpolished process if it delivers results. I don't like hierarchies. I don't like status. I won't do it. I don't like people who impose it on others. I do want to hear what people are saying. I try to be approachable.' Those are the kind of messages you can get across very powerfully.

So if the post had been for an organisation for whom hierarchy is very important, you probably wouldn't have applied or been appointed in the first place?

Possibly. So why did I go for the civil service? Good question, really. I suppose I thought I could change that. I think in the places I have worked I did have an impact, people were kind enough to say so, but I think the rest of the civil service is far too hierarchical and status-conscious. So I think you have got to make a judgement: 'Do I think I can change it?' I was younger then, and I was more arrogant and thought I could do it, but after 11 or 12 years of it I thought it was probably time to move on and let someone else have a go.

You were talking earlier about how the first six months in an organisation are often the most difficult for a leader, but also the ones with the greatest opportunity. Is it the failure to recognise this that causes certain leaders to be successful in one organisation, and to fail in the next?

Yes, I think it is one of the problems, particularly for people going from the public sector to the private or vice versa.

The culture change is too much?

Yes, I think that is one of the reasons why someone coming in, who does try to transplant a style which has grown up in a different sector or a different kind of organisation, will find it very difficult. I think you have just got to try to be good in picking out what really matters to an organization.

Respect, trust and shared values

Throughout the course of the six interviews I conducted for Six of the Best, *I had heard time and again about the importance of being yourself. Sir Michael Bichard had talked about the importance of sharing the organisation's values, and about where those values came from. I wanted to establish conclusively that the values that my other subjects talked about, such as honesty and integrity, were actually inherent in his personality.*

You were saying earlier that you are not hierarchical in any way. As a leader, is your self-image important? I don't mean image as in brand, I am talking about image in terms of how people perceive you, how people see you.

Well I am certainly trying to portray, or convey, an image which is real. This is not an image which is fabricated. I am trying to convey who I am to people. I think that's really, really important. The one thing that no leader can do without is trust. People need to feel that they know what you stand for, where you stand, and that is about the image, but image is sometimes used only in terms of something which is fabricated. I am talking about conveying what you are.

A lot of people have said to me, 'I didn't always agree with you, but I never lost respect for you. I always knew where I was with you. I trusted you. You were honest and you had integrity'. The fact that someone doesn't agree with you is second order, actually, because you never always agree with someone. The question is, can you walk away from a disagreement with a shared respect?

For example, people used to come into the departmental management meetings, and sometimes they would be shocked by the kind of passionate debate and the arguments that took place. The great thing about that team was that they didn't shy away from conflict around an issue. If there were disagreements, they disagreed, and they were able to walk away from that issue and that debate with the team intact, because it was such a passionate team which wanted to improve the quality of education, or wanted to get people back into work. And that's why there was passion. And that's fantastic. You are not scoring points off each other. You are not trying to do someone down for the sake of doing them down. You try to have an honest, grown-up debate about how you improve literacy in schools and there will be disagreements about that.

I think the leader's task is to try, in that setting, to create an environment where people do feel able to be passionate, without the team falling apart. For example, I tend to use humour quite a lot as a way of maintaining the right balance in a team. I try to use humour in a way that I think will diffuse situations, particularly when a discussion is getting a bit out of hand, or getting a bit personal. It's important that the team know each other well enough. I have spent a lot of time with teams developing their knowledge of each other and sharing the commitment of what we are trying to do. If they know each other well enough, then you can defuse a situation with a bit of humour.

I remember in the Education Department, there was a guy whom David Blunkett didn't warm to immediately. I said to

David, 'This guy's good, we must stick with him'. After about a month David took me to one side and said, 'You're right, he's the vinegar on the chips!' And that's exactly what he was on the team, and the team knew that. He didn't take it to extremes, but he was searching and was questioning, and quite challenging. And once you know that, you can cope with a lot of challenge from that person. That's the leader's task, to create this field, this stage on which people can perform and interact.

I can see how valuable humour might be, even just to defuse situations. To a prospective leader, what other tips would you offer for creating and maintaining the balance of a good team?

You do need to really understand the people you are working with, and what they are bringing to the team. People who are individual performers are sometimes brilliant. There is a point at which, however, the brilliance of their individual performance is not enough, because if you really believe that the organisation benefits from a strong team, and you have someone who just cannot be a member of that team, then I'm afraid you've just got to recognise that it's not working, and that it's not going to work.

Leaders tend not to realise that the organisation is watching. The organisation takes note of what is happening. If someone just cocks a snook at the rest of the team, bad-mouths them behind their back and think they will get away with it, then the rest of the organisation thinks that's the way in which you get to the top. I think promotion decisions in an organisation are some of the most important that a leader takes. Because people really care about their careers, and they are watching what you do when you fill posts.

In the Department, because the civil service had been dominated with the ethos that policy mattered more than delivery and management, we made a conscious effort to recruit a mix of skills. After two or three years, when we advertised for senior posts, we said that we would give preference to people who had a mix of policy and operational skills. So people who hadn't taken the opportunity to develop their operational skills were at a disadvantage, and they began to realise that we were serious. Until then, people had said that operational management was important, but had gone on promoting people who were just policy wonks.

It's the same for an organisation that says it cares about customers, but then carries on promoting people who treat customers with disdain. The organisation is watching, and reckons that customers really aren't that important. We talked about vision and values earlier, but vision and values have got to affect the way the organisation works, and what the organisation does. So if you say that customer service is important, you have to appraise people on the contribution they make to improve customer service. If you don't, then people reckon that customer service isn't important. And if you are training people, are you putting your training budget into improving customer service skills?

I spent a lot of time in the Education Department on creativity. We all talk about creativity, but there are ways in which you can help people to develop creative skills. So are you putting your training budget into that, or are you carrying on spending it on time management, and first-aid? So you have to have your vision in front of you. You have got to be constantly scanning what is happening in the organisation and question whether all of your systems are supporting that vision. Very often they are not, and the leader is in the position, more than anyone else, to do something about it. Ask yourself whether the things that make the organisation tick actually reflect the vision and the values. If they don't, then you have got to adjust it. Recruitment is obviously key. Are you recruiting the people who will have the attitudes and values that we say we want?

I get the impression that the Benefits Agency, and the Department of Education and Employment, were organisations which required formal recruitment procedures, induction procedures, appraisal procedures. But I sense that you would have preferred not to have those formal procedures in place?

No, I don't think that's right. I think I spent most of my time trying to simplify the procedures, which doesn't mean you don't have them at all. For example, I'm passionate about equality, and in order to ensure that you are recruiting in a way that delivers equality you have got to have procedures. I understand that. If you are going to have business planning, for instance, you have got to have some kind of framework, people have got to produce business plans. But I think the trick in the public sector is to try to minimise all of that bureaucracy. It does get in the way. I have seen appraisal systems which were sophisticated and intellectually defensible which got in the way of improving the organisation's performance. That is not acceptable.

The odd thing is that when you produce something like a business planning process, everyone wants to impress, and they start producing huge amounts of paper. At the university, I find that I have to tell people that I don't want lots of paper. For most issues, what I want is six sides, no more, and I want honesty about whether or not we are achieving our priorities and what the problems and issues are. Then we can have a debate around that, so it's vital not to obfuscate those issues with huge amounts of paper.

Stress and pressure

I was aware from the moment I had been introduced to Sir Michael Bichard that he seemed a very calm and relaxed person.

It is my personal view that successful leaders are able to manage their stress effectively, and I wanted to find out Sir Michael's view. Running the Benefits Agency, surely, must have been a stressful occupation?

We talked earlier about your own personal values. You come across as someone who is calm, and who manages their stress very well. Is stress an issue for you? How do you make sure that your stress doesn't impact on your team leaders, and ultimately on the rest of the team?

I do experience stress. I suppose my stress concerns whether or not I have the time that I need to give to the different organisations that I am involved in. I find that quite difficult at times. Like everyone else, I get tired. I am not as young as I was, and I am probably working longer hours than I have ever worked.

Putting that aside, I think that whether or not you are stressed depends on what you can cope with, and what you can cope with depends upon what you have been exposed to. I had a conversation once with David Puttnam, who is a friend and worked with us in the Department. We both feel that the most effective leaders are people who, as he put it, have been through the fire. When David was chair of MGM it was a hellish time, but he came out of it stronger. He knew himself better. It is a bit like training, isn't it? The more you train the more you can cope with.

I was Chief Executive of Brent Council for six years in the early 1980s when London labour politics were absolute hell. Brent was a hung council. It was probably the most difficult organisation to lead that you could imagine. People kept telling me that it's good experience, and I used to think, good experience for what? But it *was* good experience. It taught me a hell of a lot about politics. It taught me a hell of a lot about how you inspire people in the most difficult circumstances. People didn't understand what was going on. They didn't understand why the council was taking certain decisions, or why they were meeting every night until four in the morning, and changing their minds on a regular basis. And you are trying to juggle all of these things. But you come out of it a bit calmer and a bit more capable of dealing with issues. So when I went to the civil service, some of the issues that I faced were not actually that much different from Brent! So the more fire you have been through, the better equipped you are to deal with the stress and the pressure.

I see leadership as a journey, and you need to be thinking about what you are learning, and whether you are putting yourself in a position to learn. Now you may not want to put yourself into a Brent Council or an MGM, but at the other end of the scale I have seen people who carefully nurture their career so that they never lead in difficult situations. I don't want them around me because I will make mistakes, we all make mistakes, and the organisation will go through difficult times. I want people who have actually dug themselves or their organisation out of a hole.

In the civil service, I knew a brilliant young policy guy, who actually went out and ran the Harlesden Benefit Office. Now that is a bloody difficult management job. But he realised that he had been to university, he had come into the Department as a policy adviser, and yet he knew nothing about managing people on a day-to-day basis, or having to take decisions quickly without having all the information in front of him. In the Harlesden Benefit Office, someone's livelihood depends on that decision, and that brings its own pressure. And this guy came back a much better leader, much better equipped to cope with hard situations. I want people who can cope with the crises without going into freefall.

I still maintain that I learned most in my career from the eight months I spent managing an Aldi supermarket in the Midlands.

Absolutely. My daughter, who is 22 and did a degree in leisure and tourism, spent a year as duty manager at the leisure centre off the Edgware Road in London: crap building, huge staff turnover, some of whom didn't speak English, a clientele many of whom didn't speak English, equipment and resources that constantly broke down. And I was full of admiration because actually I would have found that a stretch. But she put herself in that situation and some people do that, and as a result, by the time they are 35 or 40, maybe younger, then they are pretty well the finished article. But there are others, in their 40s and 50s, whom I wouldn't want around me when the shit hits the fan.

If you're running a national organisation, and you find yourself on the front page of *The Guardian*, you've still got to keep calm under those sorts of pressures because if you don't keep calm, then you make bad decisions. And you have got to have sufficient confidence in your decision-making to make the decision that you think is right. Sometimes, you are faced with decisions where, whatever you do, you will be criticised.

For example, when I was in Brent I sacked three social workers at the end of one of the first major child abuse cases, the Jasmine Beckford case. The press and the media wanted them sacked. The council were ambivalent. Obviously, the social workers didn't want them sacked. In the end you have to go into a room and ask yourself what is the right thing to do? Forget about what everyone is telling you, and forget about the flack you are going to get. Once you have done that once or twice you feel much better equipped to take the hard decisions. Of course you ask people's opinions. You get as much information as you can in the time you've got. But you can't defend decisions you don't believe in, so you have got to take decisions that you believe in. You have got to have the confidence to do it, and be prepared to take the flack.

Presumably the emotions you have just described came to the fore during the Soham Murder Inquiry?

Quite. Yes. It's an odd thing to say, but I was lucky in the sense that what I'd done before equipped me very well to deal with the Soham Inquiry. I knew the cultures of the organisations. I had been a clerk to a police authority. I had been a solicitor. I had worked for public services. I knew the constraints under which they were working. I also had been at the receiving end of an inquiry at Brent, because the inquiry into the death of Jasmine Beckford was national news for about six months. I knew that inquiries are really bruising, damaging encounters, and that you need to get them over with as quickly as possible. The police of Humberside needed it sorted so that they could move on and continue to provide a service. So you bring all that to bear, but you can bring it to bear only if you have actually thought about those things. I think some people I observe don't reflect sufficiently. They don't reflect on what makes for a successful encounter, and what makes for an unsuccessful encounter. It's particularly important, at the end of a good day, to go home and think about why the day has gone well.

I love watching other leaders. As you probably gather, I am a great friend of David Blunkett and we worked very closely together. I have always watched David, and learned a lot from him. Sometimes it's worth thinking through why another leader took the decision that they did: what information did they use, and was it a good decision? I do that all the time with other people. I have always done that. People don't reflect enough on what works and what doesn't work, and why other people are successful, and how they make successful decisions.

Do you consciously take time out to reflect, or does it just happen?

I don't take time out, in the sense that I don't take sabbaticals. I have always involved myself in working with people and other organisations on leadership and management development activities. I talk a lot to groups of younger managers and leaders. I find that a good way to learn myself, because they challenge you. If I go and talk to a group of hungry young managers, I know that they'll want to take me apart, they'll want to challenge me, they'll want to find where I am missing something, where there are contradictions in what I have to say. That's a learning experience.

I chair the Legal Services Commission, and found it fascinating to look at how that has been led and managed, and what comparisons are to be made with the university, and what one can learn from the other. Maybe it is easier to do it if you go away for a month to the Himalayas to reflect, but I believe that I now reflect almost naturally.

Right, but if you have an immediate challenge, do you have the equivalent of going off for a ten-minute walk? Is that process in itself calming? Is it solution-providing?

Yes, I think there are some decisions that you have got to take where you do need to take a bit of time out to go and think about it, and be pretty methodical. Not everyone would do this. Some people can rely on gut instinct, possibly. But I would fairly methodically try to balance the advantages and disadvantages, the costs and benefits and try to make the best, the most rational, decision. Although in some situations you have to factor other things in, because rationality is not on its own enough.

Again, that's all about gaining experience from different situations.

We talked about stress in terms of remaining calm. I have always associated stress with inhibiting energy and creativity, and we have talked a lot about how important those two things are to a leader. Are you aware that stress is actually sapping your energy or sapping that passion, and if so, what do you do about it? Do you have something that snaps you out of it?

I don't know about that. I am not often aware of feeling under great stress except, as I say, trying to take too many things on. So in that sense it is about managing ourselves better – and having an unbelievably good secretary! That is not a cliché or an off-hand remark. Some of the worst times in my career have been having private offices or secretaries who weren't in tune with me. At times they almost deliberately seemed to make life more difficult. The best times in my life have been in the civil service where I had a private secretary, and a diary secretary, who were absolutely in tune. I remember that David Blunkett would be pretty ruthless about someone who came in and just didn't fit.

So my stress is about activity and time and it's about having someone who can minimise that for me in a way. Otherwise, I actually think you need a certain level of stress and adrenaline in order to stretch yourself and stretch the organisation, and I couldn't thrive in a place where there was none of that. Some people might accuse me of taking on some of these other roles because there isn't enough stress and adrenaline in 'just' running a university. That is probably a bit harsh.

Do you find it easy or difficult to say no? Is part of the reason that you have so much on your plate because you don't say no?

I can say no. But I find it very difficult to say no to people I owe. I mean, for example, people who have worked for me and have done a good job and have supported me. Then I find it very difficult to decline to come and do a speech for them, or something like that. The issue with speeches is that you have got to write them yourself. I was talking to Herbert Lamming recently – Lord Lamming – who has done a number of inquiries, and he was saying that one has to set standards. If I am invited to speak somewhere, then it has got to be good, and so you have got to prepare it properly. I cannot cope with people who go to a conference with two or three hundred people and they haven't prepared, because they are wasting two or three hundred hours of time there. So you have got to maintain your standards, and that means sometimes doing things like speeches for people who you owe one to.

Otherwise I'm OK saying no most of the time. I now have more excuses for saying no, because I just can't fit things in. I mean, I would take a lot of persuading to take on another inquiry like Soham, for example, because I just don't think I could cope with it with all the other things I am doing at the moment. I hadn't realised how exhausting something like that can be.

When you were asked to chair the Soham Murder Inquiry, what was your initial thought?

Well I had promised David Blunkett that if there was something he wanted me to do which was important, I would do it. So I thought it was important enough to do, really. But I now have great respect for people who chair those sorts of inquiries because it does take it out of you. I was down in my office in Holborn every weekend, and during the week. I did this job in the morning and evening and that was a killer really!

People often think that one mistake that leaders make is that they want to be liked, they want to be adored.

Has that ever been an issue for you? Do you not care?

I would rather be liked than not liked, but I don't think that's the standard you should set or measure. The standard is whether or not people trust and respect you, I think, because sometimes the conclusion you come to is that you are going to have to do some things that people won't like. You don't need to do them in a way that is unnecessarily aggressive or unpleasant, and you need to show that you understand that these things are difficult.

If there was a difficult decision that people weren't going to like, I would always try to say, 'I know you are not going to like this. I am really sorry. I have thought this one through, I have listened to what you have had to say, but I just think this is what we need to do, and I am just asking you to do it as best we can'. And I find that, by and large, people do that. So I don't curry favour. Some people don't like me, others do like me. I'm a bit abrasive sometimes, I'm a bit brusque and a bit sharp to people. But that's because I am passionate about what I do.

Small and large organisations

Earlier we talked about the challenges faced when a leader moves between the public and private sectors, or vice versa. What about leaders who move from large, corporate organisations to small ones? If you were persuaded to go and lead a team

of six people, what would you do differently? Are all the skills you have described transferable to a small organisation?

I have done it twice in the last five years, actually. I chaired one start-up company, and another near start-up company. I think the answer is that a lot of the skills are applicable, because again they are about people and clients. I think you learn a lot from different situations. I mean, I chair this consultancy company, they were all about 29 years old, and amazingly bright, really up for it. I feel a bit like the great-grand-daddy of the organisation! But that has taught me something about clients which you don't get from really big public sector organisations, in the sense that if we don't keep our clients we don't survive. So you really value your clients and you want to learn what it is that they want from you and how you can get their return business.

But that's a value, surely?

Yes, that is right. But it applies the same client focus which I have always taken very seriously, but it is doing it on a smaller scale. I think that is good for you – it is all about the learning experience. I know it's a cliché, but once you stop learning, you are not much use to anyone. I found a quote from Michelangelo, when he was 87, and he said then, 'I am still learning'. That is how people stay fresh, I think. That's why, when I was in the Department, I was so passionate about learning for older people, because I think if older people keep on learning, and are involved in some form of learning, then their independence will continue, their curiosity in the proper sense of the word will continue, they will stay younger. I think it's the same for leaders and managers. You have got to be constantly learning and taking advantages of the opportunities of going into different situations.

I haven't done a lot of private sector work in my career. I have been a non-exec, and I have chaired these two companies. I have led two local authorities, in Brent and Gloucestershire, the Next Step agency, two government departments, a university, and the Legal Services Commission. If someone asked me what I was proud of, it's the fact that I have been able to shift myself across what were quite different organisations, and apply my skills in different settings.

It sounds as if you are writing your epitaph?

Well I do think that leaders ought to be aware of the time to go, to move on. I believe that it's the role of the leader to think about succession planning. One reason I left the Department of Education was because I thought there were some really great people who could take my job, and I was delighted that one of them did and I had a hand in that. And several others have gone off to do permanent secretary and chief executive roles elsewhere. That's great. I began to feel uncomfortable, because I could see that I was in their way. I just thought it was the time to get out really. So you need to know when to move on.

I have been itching to ask this. Earlier, you described leadership as a journey. Where are you on this journey?

I personally am at the stage where I don't think I want to be a chief executive in the future. I have been a chief executive now for 26 years. That's unusual. The thing about being a chief executive is that you are the one who is always at the end of the line in accountability. I have got to the stage where I think I have had enough of that really. I think I could apply and use my skills in better ways as a chairman or in some other role. I know it sounds again like a cliché, but I don't want to be working six days a week any more, to be honest.

So when you are no longer a chief executive, what will provide the passion and the energy?

Well I would like to have a couple of chairman roles, probably in the public sector because I don't have the experience in the private sector. But I will write, I will speak, I edit things, and I will carry on doing that. I can't imagine that I am just going to disappear, but I will certainly not have the same high profile. I mean, I have turned down an awful lot of interesting things because I just haven't got time to fit them in.

The self-critic

I really thought I had established the key principles of leading people in my discussion with Sir Michael Bichard. I was building a picture of someone with vision, with integrity, and with sympathy and respect for their own values, and those of their organisation. This person gives their people real ownership of the vision, and places strong people to lead their key departments and teams. They are passionate about what they do, they communicate well, they listen, and they attempt to break down some of the obstacles that stand in the way of their people performing well. The more fire they have experienced, the better they are able to handle the stress and pressure associated with leading teams.

But Sir Michael clearly had more to say, and nothing had prepared me for what was to come.

Overall, would you say that you are a good leader?

I am incredibly self-critical. We haven't talked about that. I think the best leaders are incredibly self-critical, actually. People who know me know that one of the things I do as well as anyone is to listen. If you are a big guy with a deep voice who is fairly robust, people sometimes misunderstand that and they don't realise that you are all the time listening and picking up signals. I think I am pretty good at that. People don't spot it. I don't miss anything much. And I also think that if you are big and ugly and male, with a deep voice, people think that you are not necessarily very self-critical, and I am hugely self-critical.

So do I think I am a good leader? I do as good a job as anyone else could do in most of the situations that I have been in. So in that sense I am an arrogant leader, and yes I think I can do it as well as anyone. Do I do it well enough? Never really, because you have got to keep learning.

What form does the self-criticism take? Wishing you had done some things differently?

Oh yes. Am I going to give you examples of it?

You don't have to!

Yes, of course I think I could have done some things differently. I could have handled certain people differently, yes. I could have handled situations differently. In terms of the succession planning and team-building here, it hasn't quite worked out as planned, which is why I am staying another two years, because I want to try to leave it in a good state. The university is doing really well. But I'm not quite satisfied ... I am not satisfied yet. I think I have got to grips with management and leadership in the organisation, and have got a really good programme going now, which has had a real impact. It has been terribly well received by the 20 or 30 people who have got on the programme, and I can see, for the first time, a real interest in management. We should have started that about two years ago. It just didn't come together quickly enough. So of course there are things you could have done better.

For a lot of people, the fact that they could have done something better would gnaw away at them. Are you someone who can make the decision, accept you have done it wrong, and move on? Is that a sign of a good leader? Or perhaps it gnaws away at you too?

It does gnaw away at me really. That is why I was just pausing. I don't take mistakes well. But I think that I do have the ability to draw a line under it at the end of the day, because otherwise it destroys you and the organisation. I mean, there comes a point when you can't do much about it. You have got to learn from it. There are probably painful lessons about how you handled people or situations. If you let it destroy your confidence, then you are not going to lead. Leaders have got to have confidence.

And you are a confident person?

I am a confident person, but if that confidence spills over into arrogance then you are not a good leader.

Are you aware, in your own approach, when the definitions of confidence and arrogance become blurred?

I think I am so obsessive about *not* being arrogant that I have stopped short well before I say something and I think 'Christ, that sounds arrogant'. If I do, I am normally able to say, 'Sorry, I didn't mean to put it quite like that'.

Yes, I hate arrogance. And once you are arrogant you don't listen. That's the issue. You are so bloody cock sure, why should you listen? No one has got anything to offer you, have they? There is nothing you can learn, because you know it all! One of the problems of becoming a permanent secretary is that suddenly everyone thinks you know everything! And whereas you may be used to developing the kind of climate we were talking about earlier, where I want challenge, and foster engagement and discussion and creativity, they were just waiting there for your word. That's terrifying. That's why I need a challenging private office of staff around me. I had a fantastic private office in both the Benefits Agency and the Department of Education. You need people who can just come in and give you the bad news and the feedback that you don't necessarily want to hear.

For example, the guy who ran my private office in the Benefits Agency, Terry, is a very close friend, and is now the chief executive of a large government agency. He's just a brilliant, brilliant guy. After a while, I guess it must have been about nine months, he would come through the door and say, 'Boss, I think you should know that ...'. I remember we were going through a particularly bad time, introducing the disability allowance, which was a disaster. We had inherited it, and it had just ended up with not paying people who were terminally ill. The journalist Esther Rantzen was trying to run programmes about it, and we were running around trying to pay people before, sometimes literally, they died. After about nine months of this, I said to Terry, 'If you come through that bloody door once more and say "Boss, I think you should know that ..." I am going to kill you!'

But both he and the other people we had around us would come in and sit down and would be able to say, 'I don't think you handled that very well', or 'They are not getting the message you know', and that's vital.

Some leaders just cut themselves off. They just want to be reassured, but they don't have someone around them who can be honest with them. I don't want someone who is going to keep telling me that it is all doom and gloom, but I do want someone who is sensitive to you in the way that you have got to be sensitive to other people. That person needs to know when there is a time to give you the bit of bad news, and when actually you just need a bit of support. If you've just been on national television, and you've been asked when you are going to resign, then it's not the time to say that the unit down the road are not very happy about something. It will wait!

Inspiration

You have given me one very good example earlier, but who do you take inspiration from? Who are the leaders out there that you think tick all the boxes?

I think the people I respect most are the people who have done the job for a long time and who have consistently delivered.

I think some leaders are a bit fly-by-night really – they move here, there and everywhere and you are never quite sure whether they did actually deliver lasting change anywhere. The public sector is particularly prone to people who play around with the structures and then go before they have changed the behaviour, and you are never quite sure whether the organisation is better or worse for their having been there.

The people I respect are the people who have employed a combination of all the things I have talked about. I have mentioned David Puttnam, whom I worked with at the Department. He is someone who ticks all the boxes for me. He is great in terms of the impact he can have with people, across all ages. He can make contact with people at all sorts of different levels, he is full of ideas and creativity, and he is a real human being who cares about people.

Dennis Stevenson, who is our chancellor here at the university, is very stimulating, and also someone who has a wide range of experience. He's run Pearson, he's run the Halifax, he's run his own business. He's a strong supporter of the arts and a number of voluntary groups and organisations – I think he is great.

I don't know him, but I admire greatly Terry Leahy, CEO of Tesco, because I think he has done really well over a period of time. I admire success too. Over the last 12 months I have got to know Philip Green. You can't deny, he is an inspiration. To go into his office and see him with a group of young designers, and the way in which he still somehow manages to stay in tune with a younger generation, it's amazing really.

Change

Is leadership becoming more difficult?

Yes, I think it is getting more difficult. I think it's because the environment is changing so quickly. As a leader, you have to be keeping a close watch on what is going on out there that affects your organisation. What is going to happen in ten years' time to a university that currently stays afloat because 37 of our students are from overseas? What happens when India and China start having universities that have got the kind of reputation that our universities have got at the moment?

Leading people is changing because people are becoming more challenging – their expectations are higher, they expect more from their organisation, and clients expect more from their organisation. For example, I have noticed in five years here that what the students expect has changed and developed. They are actually paying for their education now – they are clients, and they want good services. Our website is not good enough for them. And they're right, it's not good enough! We are just doing two floors of work downstairs, because we looked like a second-rate technical college really. We weren't providing students with access to learning at weekends and, again, it just wasn't good enough. The reception area wasn't good enough, so we put money into doing that this summer. So I think the pressures are always pretty substantial in any organisation.

I sometimes say to audiences that every leader likes to think that this is the most challenging time there has ever been in the world, because it makes you feel good. Well actually there may be reasons for the current challenges, and IT must be a large part of that. IT and technology have contributed to changing expectations. A couple of weeks ago, I spoke to the Annual Conference of Forensic Scientists. They wanted me to talk about quality, and I was saying that one of the issues about quality is that it's not static. Quality is about what people expect you to deliver and from the view of the forensic scientists, DNA, for example, has changed dramatically what people expect from that profession over the last ten years. If you look at the police and the Soham inquiry, ten years ago people wouldn't have even thought it was reasonable to expect that police forces could and should exchange information. Now they expect it, and the police aren't delivering it, and so they are not yet providing quality, in my view. So technology is changing everything all of the time.

Take customer service as another example. Five years ago, an enquiry would come in by letter, and the sender would expect a seven-day response. Then fax arrived, and they would expect a same-day response. Now with email – 15 or 20 minutes is the expectation!

I don't think people should accept bad customer service from the university. Our customer service is still not good enough. We are not sufficiently consumer-focused, and part of that is because academics can be introspective. So part of my job is to try to deal with that, and to try and get everyone to understand that the most successful universities in ten years' time are probably going to be the universities that provide the best service to their students, and their graduates, and that's one of the things we have done a lot of here. We have worked much more to help our graduates when they leave to get jobs in business. I want our students to tell other people that at this university they care about you from the time you make your first contact right the way through your career.

That's a dramatic difference. What's the point of us training fashion designers and then watching most of them fail? So we now have the Centre for Fashion Enterprise, where we are taking a dozen graduates and helping them through their first two collections, giving them business advice, investing with them, taking a share in the company. It's only a small share – 10 per cent – but I found out yesterday that one of these companies, after three years, is worth six million quid!

So it is all about adapting to the changing world and changing expectations.

Innate or learned?

Are all the leadership skills we have talked about something you can learn? You are not born a leader?

Well you can learn them, yes, absolutely. I said earlier that people have different styles, and they need to find a way of being a leader in their own style. I'm probably brasher than some, but I respect quiet leaders because they probably find it easier to get people to talk to them. As I said earlier, it takes you a long time to get through the barrier of being six-foot-two and big. That is a serious issue sometimes, particularly when you are trying to develop relationships with women who are working in the organisation. I have changed my style quite a lot in 20 years. I'm not saying I have changed a lot in the last few years, because I think when I went to Lambeth and then Brent they just transformed my understanding of the issues of equality and racism, so that changed my life really. But early in my career I was certainly one of the lads and fairly brash.

I think it's important to restate that the leadership journey is about learning. I'm more confident as a leader, since I left the civil service I suppose. I think one of the most important things is people's confidence in you. You should remember that. Remember how leaders treated you. The most important role model for me was my very first chief executive at Reading because I was pretty unpolished. I was from a very working-class family and he really taught me how to behave, and he also gave me space, which I try to do with younger people too now. Back then I was too aggressive, too brash, and not someone you would want to know. But he still gave me the space. He would sit there and smile and just watch me sometimes get it wrong. He's a hero. He died a long time ago now, but he's a hero, and I try to do the same with young staff myself.

My other big influence was David Blunkett. I'd been in the civil service running the Benefits Agency for five or six years, had been Permanent Secretary for a year, but I suppose I always felt that I was an outsider, and I wasn't totally confident in that environment. Then Blunkett just came along and said, 'I've got very high standards, but you are bloody good and you and I can do great things and we are going to do great things'. And suddenly you think, 'Right, OK, I can do this!'

Do you play that conversation in your mind at times when you need a bit of an energy boost?

I think the fact that people have invested their confidence in you, if you really respect them, makes a difference to you. That's something that leaders shouldn't forget. Some leaders are so important they forget that a word from them stays with people forever.

I get really quite moved sometimes when I do these speaking engagements. This is not meant to sound self-serving, but sometimes people come up to me and say, 'You changed my life!' And I think 'Bloody hell – was it for the better?' And they remind you of a conversation which might not have figured in your life but made a huge impact on them. That's why, when you go out, you have got to be aware that you are sending messages all the time, and the best leaders know they are sending messages. They are not inhibited. Some leaders get so nervous that what they do will be misinterpreted, that they don't do anything. They are scared stiff that they will be misinterpreted and that's a tragedy really, because actually leadership can be fun, but if you're like that it's never going to be fun.

But the answer to your question is, I suppose, from the time I started working with Blunkett, which is now ten years ago, I felt confident about me as a leader. And then when you begin to reflect that you have been doing it for 26 years, you realise it hasn't been a total disaster.

It has been a huge pleasure to meet you.

I would think it's been as boring as hell.

That's the self-critic in you again!

Conclusions and recommendations

Sir Michael Bichard is an enigma. Here is a man with decades of experience of leading prominent, public sector teams, and then promoted to the highest ranks of the civil service. A man who, at the Benefits Agency, led a team of 65,000. Yet also a man who acknowledges his own self-criticism, and who all but apologised that his views on leading teams would make 'boring as hell' reading. Coming from some, this may sound or read like false modesty. But there's the enigma. Sir Michael Bichard is nothing but straight-talking, unfussy, sincere and, above all, natural. It would be hard to meet someone less prone to false modesty than him.

Despite the self-criticism, Sir Michael is charged with energy and passion for what he does. Passion is not something you can imitate, so he would advise any aspiring leader to tread a path to what they believe in or are passionate about. If you are not passionate about your organisation, your people will know. It's as simple as that. Think of leading people not in terms of motivation, but in terms of the energy that you can create in them. It's the role of a good leader to remove some of the obstacles that inhibit energy, as well as to face head-on the disagreements or issues that you might prefer to ignore.

Sir Michael talks about leading teams in terms of providing a sense of purpose and direction. This may sound like management theory, until you appreciate that he has a very specific formula that he has employed throughout his career to achieve it. Share your business vision with your people, and let them really 'own' it. Then identify and share a set of values that best represents what your organisation does, and how it does it. Leading people effectively is about vision, values and ownership. You might want to jot that down!

Respect is essential to a leader of people, and it's more straightforward than you might imagine to earn it. You 'be yourself'. If you make every attempt to convey to people what sort of person you are, then you will foster the trust and respect that every effective leader needs. Sir Michael's approach here might be summarised as being 'consistent but flexible'.

I was keen to establish the role that stress and pressure played in Sir Michael's career. I have long been of the opinion that successful leaders are people who have learned to manage their stress effectively. I was surprised by what I discovered. Sir Michael appears to thrive on pressure, and rates the people around him in terms of the fires they have been through. The more stress you have faced, the better able you are to handle it. I dare say that leading Brent Council throughout the 1980s makes most challenges seem fairly tame. Whilst Sir Michael is not suggesting that we should all throw ourselves into stressful situations with relish, he does suggest that those who have done so will make better people leaders.

Sir Michael Bichard is a hugely impressive man. Someone who has earned the respect and trust of his people throughout his career, using methods that are so simple to write down, yet so challenging to put into practice. He has a history of taking on rudderless or crisis-ridden organisations, and instilling them with a real sense of purpose and direction. He says that he is looking forward to a future filled with 'a couple of chairman roles' in his semi-retirement. Perhaps you should draft him a letter sooner rather than later?

Leading people checklist

If you lead a team of people yourself, here are some issues to think about. You might want to find a few, valuable minutes to take a clean sheet of paper and jot down any ideas that the following list generates.

Vision, values and ownership

Do you consciously try to create a sense of purpose and direction in your organisation? Does your team feel a sense of ownership for a clear business vision? Do you have a clear set of values? Does your team share your set of values? Perhaps it's time to take a fundamental look at your organisation's vision, as well as the values that you and your organisation stand for. What steps can you take to give your people genuine ownership of the vision and vales?

Be yourself

Is your role as leader an act, or are you yourself? Do your own values match up to those of your organisation? Do your people always know what you stand for? If not, think about whether it's appropriate for you to continue in your role in the long term. Perhaps it's time to find an organisation whose values match yours more closely?

Passion

Are you passionate about what you do? Do you create and enhance energy in your organisation and your people? Do you foster and encourage creativity from your people? Have you got the best team that you can around you? Is there any specific action you can take?

Communication
How well do you communicate with your people? What different communication strategies do you adopt? Could you communicate better? Do you really listen to what your people are telling you? Are you consistent, without following a dogma rigidly? Are there any obstacles that stand in your people's way that you could address right now? What action can you take?

Stress and pressure
How well do you handle stress and pressure in your role? How much fire have you had to handle in your career so far?

The self-critic
Are you a self-critic? Do you agree that being a self-critic is an important aspect of the model leader of people? What mistakes have you made? What could you have done better? What lessons have you learned from your mistakes?

The journey
Where are you on your leadership journey? What opportunities do you have for learning?

National Occupational Standards

This book covers the Providing Direction section of the NOS standards for Management and Leadership. The Table opposite will help you link these competencies to the chapters in the book. You'll also find at the end of each chapter a list of skills and an indication of the competencies associated with the material in the chapter.

Competency	Unit	Significant connection	Chapt.	Title
Develop and implement operational plans for your area of repsonsibility	B1		1	Who is this book for?
Map the environment in which your organisation operates	B2		2	What's it all about?
Develop a strategic business plan for your organisation	B3		3	Who's got the map?
Put the strategic business plan into action	B4		4	Can you see where we're going?
Provide leadership for your team	B5		5	What do we do next?
Provide leadership in your area of responsbility	B6		6	Do you take the risk?
Provide leadership for your organisation	B7		7	Can you hear me?
Ensure compliance with regulatory, ethical and social requirements	B8		8	Where do you do it?
Develop the culture of your organisation	B9		9	Who's following and why?
Manage risk	B10		10	How do you do it?
Promote equality of opportunity and diversity in your area of responsibility	B11		11	How do we do it tomorrow?
Promote equality of opportunity and diversity in your organisation	B12			

Further information and reading

Leading and leadership are popular and expanding topics – there are always new books being published and websites or blogs being launched. As a consequence, this list is not intended to be an exhaustive list of references and up-to-date publications. Rather its intention is to put flesh on the introductory material contained in this book and to launch your individual exploration of these topics. Some of the books listed are referred to in the text, other are not but are still worth reading.

Further reading

APM Earned Value Management SIG, *Earned Value Management: APM Guidelines*, 2008, Association for Project Management
APM Risk Management SIG and APM Earned Value Management SIG, *Interfacing Risk and Earned Value Management*: 1, 2008, Association for Project Management

Baguley, P, *Improve Your Project Management*, 2010, Teach Yourself

Baguley, P, *Instant Manager: Project Management*, 2008, Hodder

Baguley, P, *Instant Manager: Successful Workplace Communication*, 2009, Hodder

Belbin, M.R., *Management Teams*, 2003, Butterworth-Heinemann.

Belbin, M.R., *Team Roles at Work*, 1996, Butterworth-Heinemann.

Blake, R. and Mouton, J., *The New Managerial Grid*, 2005, Jaico Publishing

Berne, Eric, *What Do You Say After You Say Hello?*, 1975, Corgi Books

Berne, Eric, *Games People Play: The Psychology of Human Relationships*, 2010, Penguin

Bourne, M. and Bourne, P., *Instant Manager: Balanced Scorecard*, 2007, Hodder

Caruso, D. and Salovey, P., *The Emotionally Intelligent Manager: How to Develop and Use the Four Key Emotional Skills of Leadership*, 2004, Jossey Bass

Coombes, F., *Motivate Yourself and Others*, 2010, Teach Yourself

Doherty, C. and Thompson, J., *Be a Better Leader*, 2010, Hodder

Godin, S., *Tribes – we need you to lead us*, 2008, Piatkus

Gladwell, M., *The Tipping Point: How Little Things Can Make a Big Difference*, 2001, Abacus

Gladwell, M., *Outliers: The Story of Success*, 2009, Penguin

Greenleaf, R. and Spears, L., *Servant Leadership: A Journey into the Nature of Legitimate Power and Greatness*, 2002, Paulist Press International

Goleman, D., *Emotional Intelligence: Why it Can Matter More Than IQ*, 1996, Bloomsbury Publishing

Goleman, D., *Primal Leadership: Learning to Lead with Emotional Intelligence*, 2004, Harvard Business School Press

Hagel, J., Seely Brown, J. and Davison, L., *The Power of Pull*, 2010, Perseus Books

Harris, T.A., *I'm OK, You're OK*, 1995, Arrow Books

Harrison , R. and Stokes, H., *Diagnosing Organizational Culture: Instrument*, 1992, Jossey Bass

Harvard Business Review, *On Leadership*, 1998, Harvard Business School Press

Hofstede, G., *Cultures and Organizations: Software of the mind*, 1994, Profile Business

International Organisation for Standardisation, *ISO 31000:2009: Risk management – Principles and guidelines*, 2009

International Organisation for Standardisation, *ISO Guide 73:2009, Risk management vocabulary*, 2009

Katzenbach, J. and Khan, Z., *Leading Outside the Lines: How to Mobilize the Informal Organization, Energize Your Team, and Get Better Results*, 2010, Jossey Bass

Katzenbach, J. and Smith, D., *The Wisdom of Teams*, 2005, McGraw-Hill

Kellerman, B., *Followership: How Followers Are Creating Change and Changing Leaders*, 2008, Harvard Business School Press

Kelley, R., *The Power of Followership: How to Create Leaders People Want to Follow, and Followers Who Lead Themselves*, 1992, Bantam Doubleday Dell Publishing

Logan, D., King, J. and Fischer-Wright, H., *Tribal Leadership: Leveraging Natural Groups to Build a Thriving Organization*, 2008, Collins

MacLeod, D. and Clarke, N., *Engaging for Success: enhancing performance through employee engagement*, 2009, Department for Business, Innovation and Skills

Morgan, G., *Images of Organisation*, 2006, Sage

Nohria, N. and Khurana, R., *Handbook of Leadership Theory and Practice*, 2010, Harvard Business School Press

Pink, D., *Drive – The Surprising Truth About What Motivates Us*, 2009, Canongate

Peppitt, E., *Six of the Best – Lessons in Life and Leadership*, 2007, Hodder

Porter, M., *Competitive Strategy: Techniques for Analyzing Industries and Competitors*, 2004, Free Press

Ribbins, G. and Whitear, G., *Instant Manager: Body Language*, 2007, Hodder

Rogers, C., *On Becoming a Person*, 2004, *Constable*

Salter, B., *Instant Manager: Effective Presenting*, 2009, Hodder

Senge, P., *The Fifth Discipline*, 2006, Random House

Useful websites

http://www.belbin.com – Belbin website
http://www.frc.org.uk/corporate/ukcgcode.cfm – UK Financial
    Reporting Council's webpage about UK Corporate
    Governance Code
http://hbswk.hbs.edu/topics/leadership.html – Harvard Business
    School's Working Knowledge Forum on leadership
http://www.managers.org.uk – Chartered Management Institute
    website
http:// www.santafe.edu – Santa Fe Institute website
http://www.teamtechnology.co.uk – MTR-i™ team roles website
http://www.theirm.org – Institute of Risk Management website
http://www.tmsdi.co.uk – Margerison-McCann Team
    Management systems website
http://leadership.alltop.com – Top leadership news search
    website

Index